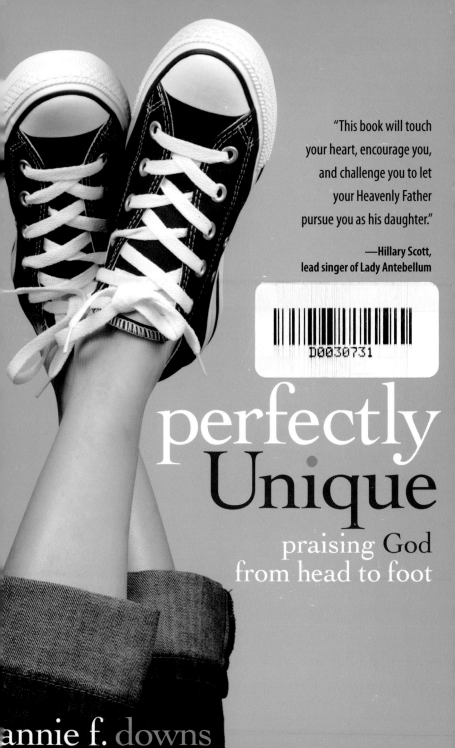

"This book will touch your heart, encourage you, and challenge you to let your Heavenly Father pursue you as his daughter."

—Hillary Scott,
lead singer of Lady Antebellum

D0030731

perfectly Unique

praising God
from head to foot

annie f. downs

Praise for Perfectly Unique

I almost hesitated reading this book in public because of the amount of laughter that comes with Annie Downs' writing. Nonetheless, it didn't matter where I was, this wasn't a book I could put down. With every chapter Annie's heart, honesty, and humor will connect you in a way that no other book has before. From "head to foot," she shows girls how to truly be confident and secure in who God has made her to be while challenging us to continue growing in that security.

—Jamie Grace
Christian recording artist and 2012 Dove Award winner
for New Artist of the Year

With winsome honesty, Annie provides clear direction and spirit-lifting encouragement in *Perfectly Unique*. She calls every woman to a place of sweet surrender so that we might accept ourselves for who we are because of whose we are. We belong to the Lord, body, soul, and spirit. Thank you, Annie, for writing this life-changing book.

—Robin Jones Gunn
bestselling author of the Christy Miller series

Annie Downs has this God-given ability to speak to you as if she's across the table from you in a coffee shop with a soy chai latte, even though you are technically reading her words on pages of paper. This book will touch your heart, encourage you, and challenge you to let your heavenly Father pursue you as His daughter. Let Him. Let your whole body glorify Him.

—Hillary Scott
lead singer of Lady Antebellum

Annie Downs brings fun to everything she touches. Her honesty is refreshing and her humorous way of looking at life will help you laugh at yourself and learn from your mistakes. She's the big sister every girl longs for, and she's the ideal companion for navigating the dramatic waters known as junior high and high school. Buy her book today—you won't regret it.

—Shannon Primicerio
Author of *The Divine Dance, God Called a Girl,* and the TrueLife Bible Study series

As a strong advocate for women owning our uniqueness, I cheer Annie Downs on with this book! *Perfectly Unique* combats the loud messages of perfection young women hear every day, speaking straight to our insecurities and showing us a new way to see our created self. I find Annie in this book like I know her to be in her everyday life: brave, honest, and fiercely funny … and it all shows up in the pages.

—Lisa Whittle
speaker, author of *Behind Those Eyes* and *{w}hole*

Annie Downs is, as we say in the South, a real character. She's quick-witted and hilarious, for sure, but she's also a phenomenal listener, an engaging speaker, and a tenderhearted storyteller. Every single one of those qualities shines through in *Perfectly Unique*, a book that speaks straight to the hearts of teenage girls. By candidly sharing her own struggles, Annie offers engaging, relatable examples that will encourage readers to trust the Lord more deeply and serve Him fearlessly in every aspect of their lives—and with every part of their being.

—Sophie Hudson
Author of *A Little Salty to Cut the Sweet*

We played "head, shoulders, knees and toes" with our little girls, encouraging them to identify and own each part of their precious God-made selves. But as our girls grew older, they began to see those same body parts through distorted lenses. Annie's beautiful book, *Perfectly Unique*, gently helps young women "baptize" each head, shoulder, knee, and toe again, reclaiming them as wonderfully, perfectly made and able to serve God while celebrating themselves and the women they are becoming.

—Sandra Byrd
author of *The One Year Be-Tween You and God: Devotions for Girls*

Annie Downs knows how to speak life-changing truth to the hearts of women. You will never see yourself the same again after reading her words.

—Holley Gerth
bestselling author of *You're Already Amazing*

Perfectly Unique is truly a unique perspective on who we are in Christ and will lead teens to the Word in meaningful ways. Annie Downs has a huge heart for teen girls and serves as a wonderful role model for teens and adults alike. I will be shouting from the rooftops about *Perfectly Unique*!

—Sarah Francis Martin
author of *Stress Point: Thriving Through Your Twenties In A Decade Of Drama*

perfectly
Unique

perfectly
Unique

praising God
from head to foot

annie f. downs

ZONDERVAN

Perfectly Unique
Copyright © 2010, 2012 by Annie F. Downs
Previously published as *From Head to Foot: All of You Living for All of Him.*

This title is also available as a Zondervan ebook.
Visit www.zondervan.com/ebooks.

Requests for information should be addressed to:
Zondervan, 3900 *Sparks Dr. SE, Grand Rapids, Michigan 49546*

Library of Congress Cataloging-in-Publication Data

Downs, Annie F., 1980-
    [From head to foot]
    Perfectly unique : praising God from head to foot / Annie F. Downs.
       p. cm.
    Originally published: From head to foot. Bloomington, IN : WestbowPress, 2010.
    ISBN 978-0-310-72434-6
    1. Young women — Religious life. 2. Young women — Conduct of life. I. Title.
  BV4551.3.D69 2012
  248.8'33 — dc23   2012030271

All Scripture quotations, unless otherwise indicated, are taken from The Holy Bible, *New International Version*®, *NIV*®. Copyright © 1973, 1978, 1984, 2011 by Biblica, Inc.® Used by permission. All rights reserved worldwide.

Scripture quotations marked (The Message) are taken from *The Message.* Copyright © 1993, 1994, 1995, 1996, 2000, 2001, 2002. Used by permission of NavPress Publishing Group.

Scripture quotations marked (NLT) are taken from the *Holy Bible, New Living Translation,* copyright © 1996, 2004. Used by permission of Tyndale House Publishers, Inc., Wheaton, Illinois 60188. All rights reserved.

Song lyrics on page 64 taken from Peter Gabriel's "In Your Eyes," copyright © 1986, Geffen Records.

Beauty and the Beast song lyrics on page 123 taken from *Beauty and the Beast*, directed by Gary Trousdale and Kirk Wise (Walt Disney Pictures, 1991), DVD.

Matt Wertz lyrics on page 197 taken from "Keep Faith," *Under Summer Sun,* copyright © 2008, Universal Republic Records.

All stories in this book are retold to the best of the author's memory. Due to the nature of some stories, certain names have been changed.

Any Internet addresses (websites, blogs, etc.) and telephone numbers in this book are offered as a resource. They are not intended in any way to be or imply an endorsement by Zondervan, nor does Zondervan vouch for the content of these sites and numbers for the life of this book.

Published in association with KLO Publishing Service, LLC (*www.KLOPublishing.com*).

Cover design: Micah Kandros Design
Cover photography: istockphoto.com
Interior design: Sarah Molegraaf

Printed in the United States of America

19 20 21 22 /DCI/ 29 28 27 26 25 24 23 22 21 20

To the She-Ra girls.
This was always for you.

Contents

Disclaimer

Dear young lady reading this book,

Okay, before you start, I need to warn you of a few things.

Annie laughs really loud. And hard. At herself.

She also loves to intercept high fives. *All* the time. (So high-five with caution when you are around her.)

She also is like a magnet. Of people. Once you meet her, there is no way you'll be able to shake her. But you probably won't mind.

She is also a tremendous human being who writes like the angels sing. Once you start this book, and meet Annie in its pages, you won't be able to stop reading.

So don't say I didn't warn you.

—Dave Barnes

Musician, comedian, with a Master's degree in the study of people, and from a certain angle has a strange resemblance to Brad Pitt('s German shepherd) (davebarnes.com)

Introduction

Our bodies are unique. No two bodies are exactly alike. Though it's rumored everyone has a twin somewhere on earth, and I kind of wish it were true, I believe God made us each individual and that we are "fearfully and wonderfully made" (Psalm 139:14).

I will say that in recent years I've made friends with two different girls who look shockingly similar. One is a mom of four from Houston; the other is a teacher in Atlanta. They speak alike and laugh alike, and I promise you that they even own the same jewelry. I've seen it with my own eyes, in all its turquoise-beaded glory. I haven't introduced them to each other. I fear what might occur. You know that scene in *The Parent Trap* where the sisters see each other for the first time? I think something along those lines might happen. Or they could begin to spontaneously fight. Which would actually be horrible. So I will let them stay in their respective states and never know about each other.

My two friends are not identical. There have slight physical differences and obvious personality differences. So there is no chance that they would be confused for each other. They are different. Each individual, each with her own story, each with her own history. Each made once.

I like the idea that God only made me once. Like paintings—there's something special about the first one. My cousin Joe is an artist, and as long as I've been alive, he has been painting. In fact, he gave me a painting, and it hangs above my bed. It's huge and purple and blue and black and weird. I love it. I asked Joe what it's like to replicate art versus painting the original piece.

The short answer he gave is that the original is work, but fun. Any copies, exact or modified, are boring, if not mindless. Creating is just problem solving, and once you solve the original problem, it's like you could train bright monkeys to do the replicating. The question is not unlike asking a chef to create the most special onion soup in the world, and after he or she has succeeded beyond any expectations, to keep making it every day.

God made you once. You were worth the work that first time. Then He threw away that mold because one of you is enough for Him. You're enough. You are the sacred painting, the original. The best bowl of onion soup in the world. (By the way, there is a recipe for amazing onion soup in the appendix.)

One of a Kind

As I think about the uniqueness of each of us, the common comparison is snowflakes. We've all heard that no two snow-flakes are alike. But the only places I've lived are Georgia and Tennessee. I don't feel good writing about anything that happens in less than fifty degrees Fahrenheit. In Georgia, we only see snow once a year, maybe twice. So I'm not the expert on the originality of every snowflake. Likewise, I can't really testify about the best snow boots or even the warmest long underwear. I can't tell you how to drive in snow and ice, and I don't personally know anyone who owns chains for their tires, though I hear that is common in other areas. To be honest, I wouldn't even know what to do if my tires had chains. It's just not that cold down here.

Maybe you aren't from the South; maybe you don't know what happens when it snows here. If we get enough to cover the grass, the news reporters are out measuring it live on camera. The world stops at the mere idea of a snowstorm. Seriously.

One February night, during my sophomore year at the University of Georgia, the weather alerts began to come across the television. Snow was coming. In a big bad nasty white way. Classes had never been canceled for winter weather, at least not as long as I had been in college. So we were glued to the television. Counties all around us were canceling school. Fingers crossed, my roommate, Candace, and I decided to embrace the idea that we wouldn't have school the next day. That consisted of such behavior as ceasing all study-related activities and screaming, "PLEASE, NO SCHOOL!" off our balcony. I know, classy. Sure enough, within the hour, the university canceled all classes due to inclement weather.

The next morning? Sunshine and in the mid-sixties. I am not kidding. It was like the storm made a complete fool of our university decision makers. The students loved it. The administration did not. In fact, if I remember correctly, we went to the park and threw the Frisbee around. On our snow day. Welcome to Georgia.

So snowflakes aren't the most common occurrence in my life. Instead, I think a better comparison of our uniqueness is blades of grass. Grass is a common denominator around the world … except of course in the desert. I've never seen two blades of grass that look exactly alike, and I've seen a lot of yards. I actually got out of my chair and walked out the back door of my house to do a little research. In my findings, based only on a small backyard and using no scientific equipment, all blades of grass seem to have a common form—straight and growing upward. But they come in different heights, widths, and shades of green. I cannot find two that seem to be exact matches. Maybe a blade of grass in my backyard and a blade of grass in the lawn of the Eiffel Tower are perfect twins, but we can never really know that, so we'll assume not.

Humans are the same way. We may come in different heights, widths, and shades (not green, of course), but we all have a common form. Aside from rare exceptions, we have two arms, two legs, two eyes, one mouth (though mine could really count as two or three—I'm loud), a backbone, skin, organs, and so on. You get my point.

God made us this way on purpose. It's no mistake that we are formed the way we are. But why? Why did God make humans in the first place?

Look at Isaiah 43:7:

"... Everyone who is called by my name, *whom I created for my glory,* whom I formed and made" (emphasis mine).

God created us for His glory. Get ready for a little Old Testament lesson: the word *create* in the original Hebrew is *bara*. When this particular word is used, God is the only subject—He does all the work. Only He can create in this particular way. We may be able to create a painting or create chaos, but as humans, we cannot *bara*. So when God made you, He did something that only He can do, and He has done that for His glory. The word *glory* here is translated *kabad* in Hebrew. This means "to bring honor or reputation, to promote something."

This short Hebrew 101 lesson does have a point. (And no, there will not be an ancient-language quiz later, unless you write one for yourself.) We look at the original language of the text to see, according to Scripture, that we were created, made especially by God, to promote Him, glorify Him, and worship Him.

The question: How do you do that?

The easy answer: You worship and glorify God by singing at church, by going to youth group and Sunday school (or some other Christian group that meets at your school), by telling Him how great He is. You glorify Him by not sinning. And that answer is correct.

But here's the better question: How do you glorify God today? Here? In the middle of your not-so-easy-to-handle life? In the everydayness you have to live?

- On Wednesday morning at school?

- On Saturday night at your boyfriend's house?

- On Tuesday morning at the breakfast table with your family?

- While sitting in a coffee shop meeting a writing deadline?

- No matter what you eat, wear, see, and touch?

- No matter where you go, whom you go with, or what you do when you're there?

- When you aren't at church or with your parents, or with your parole officer?

In all these situations, how do you glorify and honor God with your whole body? Those are the tough questions. And tough questions aren't satisfied by easy answers. Because glorifying and honoring God aren't just things we do with our mouths. We do them with our minds, eyes, ears, hearts, feet, knees, arms, and even shoulders. Our bodies were created to glorify God.

What? You don't believe me? Oh, I get it. You're thinking, *This girl doesn't know what she's talking about. My body is just a shell. Just a carrying case for my heart and mind. A good-looking shell, but a mere shell nonetheless.*

Oh ye of few memorized body scriptures! (Uh, that's me too.) Check out these verses :

> In the same way, count yourselves dead to sin but alive to God in Christ Jesus. Therefore do not let sin reign in your mortal body so that you obey its evil desires. *Do not offer the parts of your body to sin, as instruments of wickedness, but rather offer yourselves to God as those who have been brought from death to life; and offer the parts of your body to him as instruments of righteousness.* For sin shall not be your master, because you are not under law, but under grace.
>
> Romans 6:11–14 (NIV 1984 translation), emphasis mine

So the parts of our bodies should be instruments of righteousness. Interesting. Not enough proof, you say? Okay, then, try this one on for size:

> Do you not know that *your bodies are temples* of the Holy Spirit, who is in you, whom you have received from God? You are not your own; you were bought at a price. *Therefore honor God with your bodies.*
>
> 1 Corinthians 6:19–20, emphasis mine

So often when we read this passage or hear sermons on scripture, it is related to sexual purity. That's good, because (1) these verses do cover sexual purity, and (2) it's really important to choose to be sexually pure in the midst of today's culture. But honoring God with our bodies is about so much more than sexual purity. We're going to dig deeper into that idea later on.

I love this last verse. It's like the grand finale of body verses to me:

> So we make it our goal to please him [God], whether we

are at home in the body or away from it.

2 Corinthians 5:9

Our goal is to please God, whether we're at home in the body or not. If you're reading this, chances are pretty good that you are in your body. So the goal, in your body, is to please Him. We see in these scriptures that we are to honor and praise God with our bodies as a whole, as well as with the individual parts.

God Made Me

Confession: I'm not a lover of my body. I'll be the first to admit that I've had issues with my body in the past, I have issues now, and I'll probably have issues in the future.

This is just a weak spot for women. So before we go much further, you need to hear this: God *created you the way you are*. If you're going to understand the importance of glorifying God with your body, you have to be okay with your body. You are the creation; God is the Creator.

I'm not asking you to worship the creation. I'm asking you to worship the Creator. How can I ask you to honor and glorify an Artist whose work you don't consider beautiful? We're going to talk about this more in the next chapter. But be ready. If you and I really want to worship God with our bodies, we have to be at peace with ourselves. It isn't that every body issue you have is going to disappear over the next few pages, but together we will begin to unpack the heart of God in this area of our lives.

I've been amazed lately watching people's bodies (in a completely normal way, not in a stalker/awkward way). If you really think about it, it's rather unbelievable the amount of coordination and balance and skill it takes for one body to coordinate all its parts to do something as simple as get us down the street. Which is easier for some people than others.

There's a spot at my college that we nicknamed the "tripping spot." I don't know how it started, but one day I was with four of my guy friends, and as we talked between classes we watched as a stranger stubbed her toe on a break in the cement. As she tripped, she turned, looked back at the spot, and then kept walking. The next guy did the same thing.

We realized we had gathered, completely unintentionally, at a comic gold mine. So for the next few days, we met up with a singular goal: to watch people encounter this break in the cement and see their reactions. There are a few different responses that people have after they trip, stumble, or make any type of walking mistake. We got a lot of the classic *Look Back and Blame the Spot* stares, many *Ignore It Like It Never Happened* responses, and quite a few *Did Anyone See That?* look-arounds. It was heavenly. We laughed every form of laugh, and we have reminisced about it many times since then. The spot has been repaired, which is a real tragedy.

I can retell this story with no remorse, because it is common knowledge that I am not what one might call "super coordinated" either. I tripped twice today at the gym (of course) and somehow managed to get electrocuted yesterday while trying to unplug my computer. I constantly have bumps and bruises that I honestly can't remember the origin of. An acrobat I will never be. (Though I do have a deep appreciation for their skill set.) I think it is fair to say that some of us have more natural coordination than others, and those people should be in the circus.

Sitting here in the coffee shop, I watched a little girl, no more than four years old, run from the doorway and smack into the counter. Full tilt. Speed never decreasing. It was like her top half was more motivated to get there, so she leaned into it and couldn't regain control. It was, in a word, awesome. And I'm again reminded that coordination comes with time. So maybe I still have hope.

Coordination, coffee-shop sprints, and the ability to "fly through the air with the greatest of ease" aside, anyone who can move, think, jump, cry, walk, or clap—you have an amazing body.

I encourage you, before reading too much more, to take a few moments and talk to God about this idea, this thought that you look just like God wanted you to look. Because I believe He has some real truth for you, and you need to be ready to receive it. I'm not asking that you be in love with your body, but I am asking that you seek to be content with how God made you.

It's not an easy road. I'm happily thirty-two, and this acceptance journey has been a lifelong struggle. To be able to laugh about my lack of coordination is, in itself, a victory over the lies I've always believed about my body. I'm gaining ground. Every day. I pray that in this collection of words, you'll begin to see yourself as the beauty you are. But please don't stop there. Through these next few chapters, I hope you see how your body can glorify God. Your form is beautiful to Him. Declare the beauty of the Lord to the world around you. It won't always be simple; it still isn't for me. But we're working this thing out together.

So who am I to even be writing this stuff? Here's the truth. I used to be your age. I did. It's just science. There's no way around it. I was, at one point in my life, an awkward middle schooler. And a freshman in high school. I was picked on as a sophomore. I was a junior on the soccer team. I sang in the choir. I was student-body president my senior year. I was scared stiff about leaving home for college. I ate lunch in a dining hall with the other freshmen on campus. I was a youth-group intern. I overslept and missed a geography final my sophomore year. I was a youth director. I thought my life was over when I didn't get accepted into my major at college. I graduated. And every day in between? I was me, struggling to find that sweet spot of what God had planned for me *and* be who I wanted to be. To somehow bring those two goals together. All the while, fighting the lies in my head about my body, struggling to figure out where boys fit into the mix, and arguing with friends over stupid things.

So I've been there. And if you say, "Annie, you have *no idea* what it's like to be me," I say this: Nope, I don't. No one does. But I do know what it's like to be me. And I know what it's like to have friends like you. So even if we aren't exactly alike, I bet I have a friend like you. In fact, I bet I would be friends with you. So we've got that going for us, right?

Through all those years of growing up, figuring out my

own junk and realizing that maybe people didn't get me as well as they thought they did, I just needed someone to help me. To show me how to live like Christ. To look into my life and tell me what I did really well and what areas needed improvement. To somehow break down this whole Christian walk into bites that I could handle.

I know we aren't best friends (yet), but hopefully by the end of all this, you'll know what I know—we were born to be friends. And I want to give you, chapter by chapter, some thoughts I wish someone had shared with me. Bite-size thoughts.

Use this book as a reference, stick it in your book bag or on your bedside table or on a shelf. Return to it when you need it. I'd like to think that each time you read it, it's like we're sitting down at a coffee shop and catching up. I'll have a medium vanilla soy chai latte. What about you?

So I'm going to do my part. Show up for coffee (or chai, as the case may be) and tell you what I'm thinking. I'll also tell you some embarrassing stories that I'll wish you didn't know next time we run into each other in public. In return, I ask one thing of you. Be honest. Be honest with yourself, with your friends, with the women of God who encourage you and mentor you. Be honest about your body, how you praise God, and how you can improve on your praise. Know that I'm walking this road with you. Remember there is nothing I can write without first living it and knowing it to be true. I'm not going to write something I don't know.

This is grass to me, not snowflakes. (By the way, don't look for any future writings from me on raising tigers or making mozzarella cheese—I don't know anything about those things either. But gosh, I really wish I knew how to make mozzarella. That stuff is so good.)

This may not be an easy journey. I'm fully aware of that. But stick with it. I hope you laugh a little, learn something new maybe, and in the end, are better at being you. For His glory. When this journey is over, I pray you'll be able to say you are genuinely living a life of praise to God ... from head to foot.

chapter 1

All of You

I remember the first time I hated my body. Really, truly, undeniably hated it. I was in high school, though I don't remember the exact year. Freshman year, probably.

I was standing in my bedroom, in front of my oval-shaped mirror, dressing for a dinner party at our home. It's funny, some of the details are burned on my mind, like where my parents were (downstairs) and what I found under my dresser (duct tape). Other details, such as why there was a dinner party or why I had duct tape in my room are totally absent from my brain. I don't even recall the circumstances surrounding the event; I just know I wanted to be skinny. I was so angry at the fact that I wasn't the size I should have been. I honestly don't even remember what size I was. Maybe a 14 or a 16? Somewhere in there, since those are the sizes that have been my constant companions (except for a few years in college when I believed my age should directly match my pant size).

I tried on a new outfit. Jeans, I know, and a sweater. The sweater, a beautiful example of fashion in the nineties, had stripes of bright colors. It looked like rolls of different-colored play dough stacked on top of each other. I thought it was fancy and fun and beautiful. (Though to see it today would surely cause us all to bust out in laughter. Fashion is ever changing and ever leaving us embarrassed of past choices.) But sadly, it did not fit. It pulled across my roly stomach in a way that separated the play dough. Hot tears burned my eyes as I saw my own reflection. Round face. Tight sweater. Tight jeans. I was disgusting and disgusted.

Then I saw, through the blur of tears, something silver at my feet. A roll of duct tape. An evil-inspired plan quickly came to mind. I could solve this. Not only would it make me thinner for the night, it would also induce such a deep amount of pain and anguish that I would learn a lesson: *Stop being so fat, Annie.* The pain would change me, I was certain.

So I took off my sweater and began to unroll the duct tape. Starting at my waist, just below the place where my jeans sat, I wrapped myself. As tightly as I could pull the tape, I circled my body over and over. I can still hear the tape pulling off the roll as it went around and around. Crying the entire time, angry as a wet hen, I wrapped and tugged and stuffed and pulled until there was nothing on my torso except a cast of muted silver. I looked in the mirror. I was deeply angry. Angry that this was my body. Angry that it had come to this. Angry that there was no rescue from this immense amount of ugly. At the time I also had a pretty strong dislike for the way my face looked. So not only was I mad to see my body, things didn't get any better when I looked at my crying, splotchy, puffy face.

I was so angry, in fact, that I clearly remember looking in the mirror and saying, "I absolutely hate you, body." And I meant it. I made every word intentional and every word true. I wanted to make sure the message got across. Inside Annie did not like Outside Annie. Not one bit.

Thanks to my fine taping skills, I couldn't breathe, or sit. I had done quite a job on myself. My ribs felt too tight. I hurt all over. Something had gone wrong on my back; the tape had overlapped and missed some spots, which caused intense pinching. Yep, I got the message loud and clear. FAT = PAIN.

I put the sweater back on. It fit now, but there was no recovering from that moment. I couldn't go downstairs to dinner. I was unable to breathe normally. Each breath caught in my rib cage and couldn't escape. I began to worry, truthfully, that I was injuring myself permanently. I may have hated myself, but I didn't want the shame of having to tell my parents that I was hurt and needed a trip to the hospital because of a "duct tape incident." That seemed horrible.

I stood in my room for about ten minutes, dressed and taped, just staring at myself. The angry, hate-filled thoughts that buzzed through my mind were unstoppable (or so I thought). In the end, I couldn't stand it. I had to take the tape off. I was worried I might pass out, and my ribs were screaming for relief. Prisoners who committed no crime—those were my ribs. The tape, as it pulled off my pasty skin, left red streaks and adhesive. It took days for my torso to fully recover.

It took years, literally, for my heart to recover. (Has it made a full recovery? I think so.)

Learning to Love

That single event threw me to the bottom of a well. A deep, dark, smelly, moldy well built of self-hatred. And I have spent the past fifteen years slowly climbing up the sides of this well. Never many steps at once; always one brick at a time. I spent my entire high school career, and many days of college, struggling with this same issue. Now, sitting on top of the well looking back down, I grieve over the years I spent living in the bottom of that muck. But I'm loving the view from up here.

The entire time I was struggling with self-hate, I loved God. I never quit loving God. I just quit loving His creation. I quit loving all that He had made. And that "all" included me.

When Jesus was asked what the most important commandments are, His answer was very interesting.

Look at Mark 12:28–31:

One of the teachers of the law came and heard [the Sadducees] debating [with Jesus]. Noticing that Jesus had given them a good answer, he asked him, "Of all the commandments, which is the most important?"

"The most important one," answered Jesus, "is this: 'Hear, O Israel: the Lord our God, the Lord is one. Love the Lord

> your God with all your heart and with all your soul and
> with all your mind and with all your strength.' The second
> is this: *'Love your neighbor as yourself.'* There is no
> commandment greater than these" (emphasis mine).

We're supposed to love other people the same way we love ourselves. But do you love yourself? Better phrased, do you love *all* of you? Because if you and I want to live a life that reflects Christ and glorifies Him, we have to accept every part of who we are. If you want to love other people correctly, you have to figure out some way to love yourself correctly. Completely. Today. Just as you are.

Like I mentioned, this has been a long, challenging, and pain-filled road for me. It took many years of God speaking to my heart through His Word, through people, and through songs and words of encouragement before I could see I was exactly the Annie I was supposed to be.

If you're like me, even a little bit, then the idea of loving all of you seems challenging at best. More like impossible, if you were to be really honest. I sat at a coffee shop while I was writing this chapter as my friend, in tears, looked across the table and said, "How do I love me, Annie?" And as I sat there, I realized that it isn't a one-sentence answer. And it isn't a one-moment solution. I want you to know that learning to love is a process, and it takes work, just like most everything else. But as I look back on my life, going from duct-tape Annie to top-of-the-well Annie, I think there are some definite choices I had to make in order to learn to love correctly. (And I have grown to love duct tape in all its appropriate uses. But that's a whole other topic.) These five choices helped me climb out of that slimy well of self-hatred—and I think they can help you too.

1. Accept Who You Are Today

There is no amount of dieting I can do *today* to make me a size 2 by morning. No amount of plastic surgery done *today* can make me look like a supermodel by dinnertime. Who I am today is me, and God loves me deeply today. Today I have eaten okay, I went to the gym, I'm wearing sassy earrings, my hair is out of control, and I completed my to-do list. God really loves me today. Yesterday I skipped my cardio workout, had mozzarella sticks for dinner, wore flip-flops with cherries on them, and didn't spend any time reading the Bible. God really loved me yesterday, just the same as today.

I had a text conversation with a good friend today, really encouraging him to embrace where God has him. "You can do this, Jim," I texted. "Don't quit, buddy." I can love my friend well, where he is today, because I love myself today. And I can only love me because I know that God loves me—body, mind, and soul. Am I perfect? Absolutely … not. Does my body need improvements? Probably. Does my mind need improvements? Probably. Does my heart need improvements? Probably.

But I'm choosing today to love the person God made me. To look in the mirror and say, "Downs, you're all right, old girl. God loves all of you today." And then choose to make the decision to love me.

2. Identify the Lies and Call Them That!

Just because I decide that I'm going to love me today does not mean that I don't hear other thoughts in my head: "She's so skinny." "You'll never look like that." "You are such a screwup." "Your hair is out of control." (Wait, that last one is true. I ran out of product.) But the others—they're lies. I have to take the thoughts that are in my head, hold them up to the truth of what God says about me, and then decide whether to keep them or trash them.

We'll focus a lot on this when we talk about our minds. But for now, just know that you *do not* have to believe everything you hear in your head. Satan, our enemy (for real, our *enemy*), does not want you to glorify God with your body. And the best way to make sure that doesn't happen is to fill your mind with lies. As we've already established, if you hate your body, you handicap your ability to honor God with it. You aren't going to use a tool of righteousness that you dislike. So if you've always hated your hands, chances are you aren't using them to the full glory of God. If you don't want them to be seen, are you willing to reach out?

I have to wonder. What lies do you believe in your head about your body? Can you even pick them out? Can you hear the difference in their slimy gristly voice and in the voice of a God who made you exactly as you are?

3. Believe the Truth

"But how can I identify the lies, Annie? By definition, they sometimes *sound* like truth … but they aren't!" Oh, smart little grasshopper. You know all things.

My friend Jenna got a job at a bank in Nashville. She was so excited during her training when she was told that she would be learning how to identify counterfeit money. In her sassy business suit, Jenna went to work that day expecting to see and feel every different kind of counterfeit currency the FBI knew about. She loves that kind of stuff—like those shows on television dedicated to busting people doing something wrong. So Jenna had a definite bounce in her step that morning, ready to star on the next undercover show. Instead, when she arrived they sat her and the other new employees down in a room. They were each handed a stack of real money and asked to count it. Over and over. And then again. And over again. I don't know if this is totally accurate, but Jenna swears she counted the fifty one-dollar bills over one hundred times.

Frustrated, one of the other new workers asked their trainer, "Why are we doing this?"

The trainer responded, "Now you know the feel of real money. You have practiced so much with the real thing that you will easily notice the fakes."

And so is the case with identifying lies. The very best way to recognize them is to know the truth backward and forward.

Dr. Neil Anderson, in his book *Victory over the Darkness* (Regal Books, 1990), made the following list of who we are in Christ. It's a long list of scriptures. I like to use it as a reference, something I look back on whenever I need a reminder of what's true about me. And to make your life a little easier, I've summarized what each verse could be saying to you. Of course, you should also read the Bible itself to see what speaks to you. But for starters, I'd suggest using it in your quiet times with God. Pick a few of the verses and write them out in your journal. Then look at each verse as a promise God makes to you. Here are a few examples:

- *John 1:12* . . . . "Annie is God's child."

- *John 15:15* . . . . "Because I am a disciple, I am a friend of Jesus. I am!"

After you write down these statements, start reading them out loud to yourself. Learn and hear and write the truth. That way the lies will feel completely different.

Who I Am in Christ

I am accepted ...

- John 1:12 . . . . I am God's child.

- John 15:15 . . . . I'm the kind of girl that Jesus is friends with.

- Romans 5:1 . . . . I am justified. Just as if I'd never sinned.

- 1 Corinthians 6:17 . . . . I am one with Christ through the Holy Spirit.

- 1 Corinthians 6:19–20 . . I have been bought with a price and I belong to God.

- 1 Corinthians 12:27 . . . I am part of Christ's body.

- Ephesians 1:3–8 . . . . . . I am a child of God. Really. Adopted. In the family.

- Colossians 1:13–14 . . . . God has rescued me from darkness, redeemed me, and forgiven all my sins.

- Colossians 2:9–10 . . . . I am complete in Christ.

- Hebrews 4:14–16 . . . . . Because of Jesus, I have access to the throne of God.

I am secure . . .

- Romans 8:1–2 . . . . No condemnation for me—I'm free of it!

- Romans 8:28 . . . . I can be sure that God is working everything together for good.

- Romans 8:31–39 . . . . . . I can't be separated from the love of God.

- 2 Corinthians 1:21–22 . . I have been established, anointed, and sealed by God.

- Philippians 1:6 . . . . God is going to complete every good work He starts in me.

- Philippians 3:20 . . . . . . I am a citizen of heaven.

- Colossians 3:1–4 . . . . . I am hidden with Christ in God.

- 2 Timothy 1:7 . . . . I don't have to be afraid—I have a spirit of power, love, and a sound mind.

- 1 John 5:18 . . . . The evil one cannot touch me—I am born of God.

I am significant . . .

- John 15:5 . . . . I'm a branch. Jesus is the vine. He gives me life.

- John 15:16 . . . . I will bear good fruit.

- 1 Corinthians 3:16 . . . . I am God's temple.

- 2 Corinthians 5:17–21 . . I am a minister of reconciliation for God.

- Ephesians 2:6 . . . . God raises me up, and I'm seated with Christ.

- Ephesians 2:10 . . . . God made me on purpose.

- Ephesians 3:12 . . . . Because of Jesus, I can be confident when I go to God.

- Philippians 4:13 . . . . . . I can do all things through Christ. He gives me the strength I need.

Work on What You Can

All this being said, loving yourself also means taking care of yourself. It took me too many years to figure out this truth. For most of my life, I didn't wear trendy clothes or cut my hair in cute styles. I told people it was because I'd rather be comfortable. And to some extent, that was true. But the truest answer is that I didn't feel like I deserved to be cute. To be attractive.

But if you really love yourself, you display that on the outside. Not that you have to spend tons of money on expensive jeans or buy top-end jewelry, but it is important to be on the outside who you know you are on the inside. Let the world see that you are learning to love well, starting with how you treat yourself. Because I know that God loves me unconditionally, I've learned how to love myself and who He made me. And by working on that every day, it gets easier and easier.

Here are six tips on how you could outwardly display to the world that you love yourself:

1. Exercise. Your size isn't the issue. There isn't a pretty size or an ugly size. There is a point at which you become unhealthy and your body suffers. Exercise doesn't have to consist of running a marathon, unless that's something you want to do. (I have no clue why that would be "fun," but if it makes you happy, go for it.) Just go on a walk. Join a gym or a recreational sports team. Just get out there and move your body.

2. Eat Right. I have a deep love for all things ice cream. Mix it with chocolate-chip cookie dough and I'm on cloud nine. It's the epitome of delicious. But I can't eat ice cream for breakfast, lunch, and dinner. Not for a lack of skill or desire—I have the determination and the want to pull that off. But I know it isn't healthy for my body, and so I choose to eat it maybe once a week or once a month. Moderation is key, girls. Moderation. And prayer. Weird? Maybe. But trust me that when you sit down and ask the Lord to direct how you eat, He will. I have grown to love my body, to love the way the Lord made me, so I can't imagine filling my body with food or drink that will destroy it. I try to choose the things that will honor my body and represent the Lord well.

3. *Buy Cute Earrings.* Or bracelets. Or necklaces. Or rings. Or toe rings. Or brooches, like my grandmother. That classic look is coming back, or so she keeps telling me. Again, I'm not saying spend a lot of money. Just add some sassy jewelry to your wardrobe. Need help? Ask someone who reeks of sass. A girl whose fashion sense you respect greatly. Get her to go with you to a store and help you buy one thing.

4. *Wear at Least a Little Makeup.* Again, this is where some help is good—from your mom, or a mentor, or a friend who has makeup-wearing tactics that are phenomenal. Don't put makeup on like you're icing a cake. It shouldn't be a layer. But use the products that are out there to enhance the beauty that the Lord has already given you. Remember, it is all about making your outsides reflect the beauty that is on the inside. It's also about showing the world you're beautiful, and you know it. This isn't for other people—it's for you. For you to see on the outside the beauty you have on the inside.

5. *Pluck or Wax Your Eyebrows.* My mom told me to do this

when I was in college, and I got highly, *highly* offended. I did not care what my eyebrows looked like. I fought it until my room-mate talked me into doing it. It didn't feel awesome—obviously. But my eyebrows looked great. Once it was done, I was hooked. I can't believe I'm saying this, but my mother was right. My face really did look better with well-sculpted eyebrows.

In fact, when I went this past Thursday to get my eyebrows waxed, the beautician said something rather interesting in her thick Russian accent: "Your eyes are beautiful, but you have to bring the beauty out by framing them beautifully. Beautiful brows equal beautiful eyes." I also had her wax my, ahem, mus-tache. Don't get me started. I can't believe that I even have hair growing over my lip, but it's true and it has to go. Wax it, ladies.

6. *Get Enough Sleep.* Just do. It will make your face look better and it will make you be nicer to your friends and fam-ily. Sleep rejuvenates your body. I'm quite the accomplished sleeper—I love going to bed early and staying in bed late. I love to take naps (which I like to call "snoozle mcdoozles"—and no, I don't remember why). So this isn't a challenge for me. But it may be for you. Make a choice to get enough sleep. To live up to your potential in Christ, you have to have rest.

Focus Your Attention on the Inside

This is where we'll camp. Because if your heart, your soul, your spirit aren't in line with who God wants you to be, then fixing up the outside is pointless. Who you are on the outside should be a reflection of what's on the inside. Your "knower," as I like to call it. If you have accepted Jesus into your heart and He is your Savior, then by the power of His death and resurrection, you are clean. And you can be grateful for that. But more than being clean, do you want to be holy? To live in a way that glorifies God? We want our bodies to be instruments of righteousness (Romans 6:13).

This is a lot of information, I know. But use it as a resource. Don't go changing every area of your life tomorrow. People will be weirded out, and you will be exhausted, trying to be someone you're not. These are the steps that worked for me and many of the women I have talked with. Embrace them slowly but surely. Choose to love yourself not because of who you are but because of Who made you. And then live in a way that honors Him.

Maybe today you just need to be able to say that you are okay with how He made you. Maybe there is no "love" yet. That's fine. Just take a step. One of my favorite Faith Hill songs, "This Is Me," says, "I'm just like everybody else. I try to love Jesus and myself."

And that's all we can do. Try. Just try to love Jesus. And yourself. In that order.

chew on this

Ponder:

> What are your best qualities?
>
> What kind of lies are you hearing in your head?
>
> Who do you trust to talk through this stuff with?

Read: Psalm 139

Look up: *beautiful, lovely*

Do it:

> Take out your journal and write down a few of the things
> you already really like about yourself. Then list a few of the
> areas in which you hope to improve—not necessarily your
> body itself but ways you want to improve in how you treat
> the body God has given you.

chapter 2

Mind

I loved third grade. For some reason, probably because of my awesome teacher, Mrs. Albers, third grade holds many vibrant memories. For example, I remember wearing just a long T-shirt with a belt around it, like a dress. Laugh if you will, but know that was relatively cool in the 1980s. (And call me crazy, but isn't that getting to be cool again? If only I could find that teddy bear T-shirt ...) I also remember bringing a gallon milk jug to school to make into a space helmet. We got to lie down on the floor and pretend to be astronauts. Other students would spin the globe, stop it with one finger, and tell the astronauts where on Earth they had landed when they returned from their space trip. I also remember looking up cuss words in the dictionary and sitting next to my boyfriend, Josh, at lunch.

But one of the memories that sticks out to me the most was a video we watched about the human body. Bizarrely enough, I remember watching it in the classroom across the hall. The video was showing how the nervous system and brain worked. It was a cartoon, and there were thousands of little worker men inside the body. They looked, in my memory, like Mario and Luigi from Nintendo. So these little men would run up and down the cartoon body sending messages back and forth. And the men in the brain worked the hardest. They were constantly sending out messengers to different parts of the body—if there was an injury, they sent an ambulance; if there was a sickness, they sent an army; and so on. It's amazing the clarity with which I remember a video from honestly more than twenty years ago (and that's freaky in itself). I remember thinking that I wished the video were true to life—I would have loved to know that there were thousands of Marios and Luigis running through my body keeping everything in check. I'm kinda strange like that.

As I've thought about this memory, I believe the Lord has given me a reason why the experience is so crystal clear to me. When it comes to our minds, God desperately wants us to understand their importance and power, so He's letting me remember this silly video because of the main lesson I took from it: everything else depends on the working of the mind. It's been said that every injury is a brain injury. The nerve endings all over your body, whenever hurt, send a message to your mind to make sure your brain is aware that there's a serious *ouch* somewhere. So although it may be your finger that was burned, without your mind indicating that *ouch*, there would, in essence, be no *ouch*.

How many times have you heard of a brain transplant? Now I'm no doctor, but I know that a brain transplant is virtually impossible. The brain is the core organ of a human body. You can have a heart transplant, leg or arm transplant, even a lung transplant. But there is no substitution for the brain God has given you. Your mind is yours alone, and it always will be.

Our imaginations are amazing. Just think: every book, television show, movie, song, piece of furniture, street design, pair of flip-flops—everything—was once an idea. Simply a thought in someone's brain. And because your brain is so important— all of your genius math equations, famous quotes, and fashion sense are housed there—it's vital that you protect it. First and foremost. At any point of the day, your mind is full. It is up to you what fills your mind and what doesn't.

So what is on your mind right now? Here are the thoughts that are in *my* head this very minute ('cause I'm sure you're just on the edge of your seat in anticipation):

1. A great song is playing on my iTunes.

2. Some guy I'm supposed to know just came into the coffee shop.

3. Do I stop listening to this song and say hi?

4. Why is my right foot so cold, but my left foot isn't?

5. This is by no means the best chai latte I've ever had.

6. Why is the wireless internet not working?

7. Did anyone just see me mouth the words to this song? Because that's a bit embarrassing.

8. That guy has a lot of beard hair. A lot.

9. Pine cones.

I'm going to stop there because I fear exploring this much more could get uncomfortable. The point is that my mind is full. And weird. Your mind is full. Hopefully less weird.

Homecoming Queen

This chapter has a special place in my heart. Because I think, when all is said and done, this may have been the chapter that would have changed my life as a young woman. I lived for the majority of my life with the understanding that whatever I heard in my head was true. If I heard "You look cute," then I was cute that day. If I heard "You are an ugly cow," which was common, then I believed it. I don't recall anyone ever telling me that what I heard in my head wasn't necessarily true. I thought that my mind was a locked box and I was the lone key holder. So if it was in my head, by gosh, it was true.

My senior year of high school, I was on the homecoming court. We didn't have a football team, so the crowning of the homecoming queen happened at halftime of the boys' basketball game. The dress I found was a beautiful deep purple, and it was *loaded* with purple and silver sequin beads. I'm telling you, that dress was so heavy I can still feel the weight of it on my shoulders. I liked it a lot.

I wish I could say that I loved it. I think if I found that dress today, I would gush over how gorgeous it is and how smokin' hot I look in it. But my brain was so full of lies at the time that I honestly don't remember, even once, thinking I looked pretty. There were days when I thought I was decent (like the night of the homecoming game), but I don't once remember thinking I was really pretty.

When it came time to crown the homecoming queen, I almost fell over when they called my name. Me. Annie Downs. The ugly, fat girl just won homecoming queen? I teared up and waved and forgot to hug my daddy. I held the flowers and smiled for the newspaper photographer.

And when I got home I cried. All by myself, lying on my bed, still wearing that heavy beaded dress. Because in my mind, I heard this: *You won because everyone felt sorry for you. They voted for you because you're ugly, not pretty.* So instead of being proud of the fact that I had been crowned, instead of enjoying the moment and savoring it, I hated it. I was embarrassed and I didn't want to see my friends the next night at the dance. I was sure they had all discussed it behind my back and felt sorry for me because I was so ugly.

Now, without even having been my friend in high school or seeing a picture of me in the beautiful purple dress, you can hear how ridiculous those thoughts were, right? They were lie upon lie upon lie. John 10:10 says, "The thief [Satan] comes only to steal and kill and destroy." And that's exactly what he did to me that winter night in 1998—he stole my excitement, he killed my hopes, and he destroyed my self-esteem. I can never get that night back. I can never recover the pieces of my heart that were broken that day. Oh the things I would say to Homecoming Queen Annie if she were standing here in front of me!

But the redemption of that moment won't be found in talking to a younger version of myself. The real victory is that *you* are hearing this story, and I pray that you can make different choices with your mind than I did with mine.

Because your mind isn't a locked box. It's more like a superhighway, with hundreds and thousands of cars driving on it every day. Your job, as the keeper of your mind, is to know which of those cars to keep and which ones to let drive right out the other ear. Identify truth. That's the key. (We've talked about that a lot already—remember the counterfeit-money story?)

Guarding the Palace

Your sweet mind. It's just a container. But a fragile container, don't forget. So your first duty with your brain it to protect it. Things are going to fill it. That's just the nature of your mind. It's up to you to decide what gets to fill that container.

Have you ever seen the changing of the guard at Buckingham Palace in London? It's a rather pompous affair, but cool, no doubt. Every day people gather outside of the palace to watch as the guards switch positions. Though the Queen of England is nowhere in sight, every day without fail, there are guards standing at every entrance to the palace. Why? Because protecting the queen doesn't simply mean protecting whatever room she is in at the moment. To protect the queen, the guards must protect all the entrances to the palace as well.

So it is with your mind. To protect your mind, the Queen Brain, you must stand guard at the gates. What are those gates? What are the portals to your mind? Your eyes. Your ears. Those are the places you need to guard. (We'll talk more about those in later chapters.) Yet even if you're careful about what you watch and what you hear, the Enemy will still whisper lies to you, trying to convince you to sin or doubt or question God and His love. So don't despair! Hearing lies in your head is *not your fault*. It's the nature of being human, especially being the kind of human who loves God.

So, what? Is the fight hopeless? Absolutely not! I think there are ways we can win the battle in our minds and learn to glorify God with them. Because I used to teach elementary school, silly memory games come into my head all the time. It is almost like they create themselves. So it is with the ways we can glorify God with our minds. In fact, we're going to learn a little acrostic, using the letters M-I-N-D. It's kind of like a cheer, so feel free to yell this out at any time. I'm not responsible for the reactions of the people around you, but I'll be honest and say I totally wish I could hear you do it. 'Cause that kind of stuff is awesome to me. Ready? Go!

M = Mute the Lies!

The first step to winning the mind battle is to mute the lies. Literally quit listening to them. The only way to do that is to identify whether something is a lie or the truth. But how? You have to study the Scriptures and know what is true. Only then can you call a lie a lie and choose not to believe it.

Once you know something is a lie, you have to choose to quit believing it. Right now I'm single. But in my heart, I really want to be married one day. And I believe that God gives us the desires of our hearts. A lie that Satan likes to feed me often is "No one is ever going to marry you—you aren't pretty enough." Some days it makes me cry. But most days, when I hear that lie, I think, "No. That is *not* true. And I won't hear it." And then I kind of do something silly.

I imagine myself standing at home plate on a baseball field. I imagine those words, all jumbled together in a baseball. Then I picture someone pitching the lie ball to me, and I hit it and score a home run. The ball goes over the wall and out of sight. Is that ridiculous or what? I know, totally silly. But it helps me. In my mind's eye, as I see that ball fly out of the outfield, I remember how true God is and the reality of His love for me.

But it is a choice, every time.

You *have* to mute the lies. The whisperer won't quit whispering. The same goes for the temptation to sin—it isn't going to end just because you decide you don't want to hear it. In fact, it may get worse.

While I've been writing this chapter, ungodly and untrue thoughts have been flooding my head like a rushing river. And I just have to keep muting them, playing baseball, and then trying to glorify God with my mind. Do you know what keeps me going? My love for God and my thoughts of you. You, the sweet friend on the other side of this page, who is desperate for some relief from the lies in your head. There is freedom for you.

Look at this verse:

> We demolish arguments and every pretension that sets itself up against the knowledge of God, and *we take captive every thought* to make it obedient to Christ.
>
> 2 Corinthians 10:5, emphasis mine

Taking captive every thought is exactly what we've already discussed. Look at every thought that comes through your head that could possibly be a lie or a temptation, and make it obedient to Christ. You may even want to say that out loud: "Thought—you are not the truth. My mind is choosing to be obedient to Christ."

Yes, you may feel silly doing it, talking out loud to yourself and all. But listen, is it worth it to be free from the lies? Homecoming Queen Annie would have said yes.

I = Invite the Truth!

Looking back on that night I was crowned homecoming queen, I can only imagine how different things would have been had I known the truth. Verses like Song of Songs 4:7 that says, "You are all beautiful …; there is no flaw in you." Or what if I had taken time to read Psalm 139:13–18? And believed it?

> For you created my inmost being; you knit me together in my mother's womb. I praise you because I am fearfully and wonderfully made; your works are wonderful, I know that full well. My frame was not hidden from you when I was made in the secret place. When I was woven together in the depths of the earth. Your eyes saw my unformed body; all the days ordained for me were written in your book before one of them came to be.

How precious to me are your thoughts, God! How vast
is the sum of them! Were I to count them, they would
outnumber the grains of sand— When I awake, I am still
with you.

Now, as a girl with a healed mind, that scripture means the
world to me. God knit me together. I am wonderfully made. He
has so many loving thoughts toward me that it would take up
beaches and beaches if we counted them.

You must invite this truth into your noggin. You have to
make space for it, which is all the more reason that you should
hit those lies out of the ballpark. If your mind is a container—
and it is—one step toward winning the battle is to remove the
lies and replace them with truth.

When I was in college, the girl who discipled me, Anna,
had me do an exercise that I recommend to you. Grab a hand-
ful of note cards, your Bible, and a pen. On each note card,
write a different lie that you hear in your head, or a temptation
that seems too strong. If you don't know what to write down,
just pray and ask God to make it clear. Ask Him to show you
what you believe that isn't true. Here are some examples:

- "I am ugly."

- "If I don't sleep with him, I don't love him."

- "God is mad at me."

- "God loves [*fill in the blank*] more than He loves me."

And the list could keep going. Mine did. Sitting in Anna's
apartment, I wrote and wrote. Sometimes I would say one out
loud to her: "Anna, if I hear that I am disappointing God by not

losing weight, is that true or not?" Because sometimes you need some help knowing the difference between true and false. So ask! "That is a lie," Anna would respond, so I would write it down.

In the end, I had more than twenty-five note cards with lies written on the front of them. And over the next few weeks and months, I added to that list as I prayed and lies were revealed. Then Anna had me do something really interesting. For each card, each lie, I had to flip the card over and find a matching verse that said the truth. And I had to write the whole scripture out. Because I like colors, I wrote the lies in black and the truths in green. I have my cards sitting right here (eight years after making them!), so I'm going to give you some personal examples:

LIE: I will never be physically who God wants me to be.

TRUTH: 1 Timothy 4:8—"For physical training is of some value, but godliness has value for all things, holding promise for both the present life and the life to come."

LIE: God picks other people over me.

TRUTH: Deuteronomy 10:17—"For the LORD your God is God of gods and Lord of lords, the great God, mighty and awesome, who shows no partiality and accepts no bribes."

LIE: I am not disciplined enough to hear God's voice.

TRUTH: Isaiah 30:21—"Whether you turn to the right or to the left, your ears will hear a voice behind you, saying, 'This is the way; walk in it.'"

See how it works? And I still use the cards all the time. Because, like I said, the accuser doesn't stop accusing, the liar doesn't stop lying. He continues to try to steal, kill, and destroy. But when you *mute the lies* and then *invite the truth*, you're protecting your mind from his attacks. And allowing God to speak truth to you.

N = Notice the Patterns!

This step in defeating the lies is really important to me. Because sometimes it's easy to predict when Satan is going to start in on you, and at those times, your cards should never be far from your side. For example, in my own life, I know that around the holidays, I'll have to fight the untrue thoughts regarding my future. And during that certain time of the month (ahem, you know what I mean, right?), I am always going to hear negative thoughts about my body. So I'm ready for them.

This takes time. It takes being willing to invest in your own mind's health and paying attention. And truthfully, this comes with struggling and giving in to the temptations and the lies and then saying, "Wait a minute ... How did I get here? I thought I quit believing that. Didn't I stop struggling with that?" Soon enough, you begin to see the patterns. When you can see the battle coming, you are better prepared. Does that mean that you'll never fail? Nope. Or that you'll never believe another lie? Nope. I still struggle from time to time. But when I'm noticing a pattern (Oh, it's Christmas!), then I'm able to identify the lie more quickly (No wonder I keep hearing that I'll be alone forever—Satan is trying to steal my joy and my hope!), and I'm able to tell myself the truth (God promises me a hope and a future in Jeremiah 29:11!).

D = Decide What You Think!

Some things need to stay in your mind forever. Things like your convictions, scriptures, my birthday (July 7)—you know, the life-changing things. But seriously, you need to decide what you think and stick to it. That's the fourth step in defeating Satan's lies.

What are your convictions in dating? In friendships? What are the boundaries you have with time on the computer? In front of the television? At the gym? What scriptures from your cards need to be in your mind all the time? Because you should be memorizing them.

One of my students, Macey, was having a hard time when she was in my class in fifth grade. She was troubled by some decisions her friends were making, and she asked me how to pick good friends. I showed her Proverbs 13:20:

> Walk with the wise and become wise, for a companion of fools suffers harm.

Now that Macey is a senior in high school, her life is shaped by this verse. She memorized it (we both did), and in the past seven years made choices based on the truth of this verse. You can see it in her life—in her friendships, in her relationships with boys, in her decision making. Macey isn't perfect. But she made a decision to live by what God's Word said, and day by day she continues to stick to that decision.

I want to be like Macey. I want to hide God's Word so deep in my heart that my life truly reflects Scripture.

Repeat with me (in a cheery singsong voice, please):

M—Mute the Lies!

I—Invite the Truth!

N—Notice the Patterns!

D—Decide What You Think!

So, how do you feel about the cheer? Nice, huh? And trust me, I know that is *a lot* of information to absorb. Don't get stressed and overwhelmed. Give yourself time, read this section over again in a few days, and get started on your Lie and Truth cards. Also, talk with adults or mentors or other people in your life whose walk with Christ you respect. Never be embarrassed to talk about the lies you hear or the truths you want to cling to. God has placed mature women in your life for you to go and talk through this stuff with. And if He hasn't, pray He'll send them. And email me.

The best part of all this is that your mind, at the same time, can do *so many* good things for you. Use it well—create beautiful things, follow through with great ideas, love people who pop into your mind. If you have accepted Jesus as your Lord and Savior, the Holy Spirit lives in you. *All* of you. That includes your mind. All your favorite artists, writers, sculptors, decorators, chefs, and musicians first create the things you love in their minds. And you can do the same.

What kind of amazing ideas are lurking up there in your thoughts? Could you write a book to inspire a generation? Can you draw that picture you see in your head and give it as a gift? Do you have a recipe that would blow your friends' minds? Are you a mathematical genius who might be able to help your church with their budget? Is there some sort of business you want to start? Do it! If God has put the sparks of an idea into your mind, it's up to *you* to follow through.

I'm praying for you today. I'm praying that you would have the mind of Christ. That as you seek to make your mind an instrument of righteousness, you would be able to identify the lies, believe the truth, and change this world with the ideas in your mind that can become reality.

chew on this

Ponder:

What lies do you hear in your head?

What is the truth that you should cling to?

Do you notice any patterns in your life that tempt you to believe certain lies?

What have you decided to keep in your mind?

What is one thought, one idea in your head that you think God may have put there?

Read: Psalm 139:17; 1 Corinthians 2:16

Look up: *mind, thoughts*

Do it:

Take some time today and make your Lie and Truth cards. You can find them in the back of this book, ready to be cut out and used. Remember that on the front of each card, you'll write a lie that you hear in your head. On the back, write a scripture verse that defeats that lie. Then share your cards with your parents or a trusted mentor.

chapter 3

Eyes

I don't treat my eyes very well. I have the distinct feeling that I'm really going to regret it someday. I don't see well; in fact, I'm legally blind. Which is a fun fact that I often use in the game "Two Lies and a Truth." I have worn glasses since sometime in elementary school. I thought I was the cool kid for having glasses. I know, I was a bit delusional. Now as a mature, cool adult, I wear contact lenses. I don't take them out as often as I should. As in, I could go a month and totally forget that these aren't my real eyes; that in fact a piece of plastic is living in my eye sockets, and not taking them out every night isn't healthy. Sometimes I wake up in the mornings and I can't open my eyes all the way. I call it "frozen contacts." Because it feels like they're frozen to my eyeballs. I can't see anything—every object is fuzzy, and it takes ten or so minutes of strained blinking to be able to see clearly. To be able to focus.

I'm always a little afraid to ask the doctor why I should take out my contacts. I just don't want him to say, "Well, if you sleep in them too much, your eyes will possibly fall out." Or something equally as devastating and likely. But doing a bit of research, I have found that one of the major problems is that our eyes need oxygen. And wearing contacts too long can make red blood vessels pop up all over each eye. That sounds gross.

(I'm feeling very convicted right now, by the way, so don't concern yourself. I'll take them out tonight.)

When I talk about glorifying God with our eyes, that probably includes taking my contacts out like my doctor instructs. I hear ya. But in reality, it's all about our focus. That's all there is to it. Where we look, where our eyes are, is where we are focused. And that focus determines the recipient of our praise.

I think that's why I can get stuck on Facebook for an hour and a half when I should be, oh, I don't know … writing! Because I literally can't take my eyes off it. It has my full attention. Just today, I located what one might consider a Facebook treasure—a gem of sorts. After much searching (I'm known as a rather skilled Facebook friend-finder), I found one of the football players I adored in high school. I haven't seen him since he graduated (1996), except once in Walmart. Now to see his face, read all about his life, check out all of his friends—it's almost too much. And I wasted a lot of time online. Somehow the past ninety minutes just ticked away like it was no big deal, and I didn't even notice. My eyes were occupied, so my mind was occupied.

I can do the same thing with the television. Oh! Series marathons on television were a killer in college. I could waste nine hours on a beautiful Saturday just watching *Full House*. Besides that, there are Food Network marathons, and shows like *What Not to Wear* and *Dog the Bounty Hunter*. And a personal favorite of mine, the *Colonial House* series on PBS (or *Frontier House*, *Texas Ranch House*, or *The 1900 House*—I'm not picky). Don't judge me; that television series is a gold mine of awesome. You've missed out if you haven't experienced people today pretending to live in another decade or century. Sure, I'm the only one of my friends who will even consider watching it, but I have no shame. I love PBS! I don't care if the whole world knows it. Any type of television, not just public broadcasting, sucks me in and steals my time by first grabbing my eyes and then getting my attention.

I remember a couple of years ago I was teaching fifth graders about idioms, and I tried to teach my class what "He catches my eye" means. I explained how it isn't someone literally catching your eye; instead, it means to take hold of your full attention. Then I used an Atlanta Falcons football player as an example: "Matt Jackson catches my eye."[1] They got it, we all laughed, we moved on.

Fast-forward to two months later when I was going to meet said Falcon player. I totally dressed up and wore the cutest shade of lipstick that has ever existed. (He was single at the time—now he's married with kids, and I wish him all the luck

---

1. His name is changed here, by the way, so don't try googling it. But trust me, the guy is attractive.

in the world. But I promise I wasn't dressing up for a married dude.) My students made a huge card. I took it along to give him. As I set it on the table in front of him and he opened it, I saw, glaring at me from the bottom right corner in bold black letters, "You catch my teacher's eye."

Have mercy! Get me out of here. Way to go, kids. You sure got the concept. And you used it in context. Congratulations.

I was mortified. Awesome lipstick or not, the truth was revealed—I'm a dork. And a superfan.

Embarrassing stories aside (please?), eyes fascinate me. Not just the fact that they have such a direct connection to your brain (even though they do), but also the idea that eyes are so expressive and so important when you're talking and listening. Is there any more obvious sign that someone is ready to leave a conversation than when they start looking around? And you can always tell if a dude is interested in you based on how deeply he looks into your eyes. Right? Mmm … that's a nice feeling.

Focus. I'm losing it.

Your eyes are a constant variable in every situation you're in. (Except sleep, I guess.) In fact, I was just sitting in Starbucks reading when a couple of people came in and sat down right in my line of vision. I was completely distracted by them and their conversation. Even though my iPod was playing in my ears, if my eyes were on them, I could hear every word they said. Interestingly enough, if my eyes were on the book I was reading, I was oblivious that they were there. I was almost experimenting to see if I could jump in and out of their conversation—read a paragraph, eavesdrop, paragraph, eavesdrop. It takes very little to entertain me. And trust me, it was all I could do not to ask

annie f. downs

him why he even bought the motorcycle, since it's January. (By the way, she wasn't happy about it either.)

Amazing how the Lord made us, isn't it? It almost seems that the rest of our bodies respond to what our eyes do. Our minds take in what our eyes see.

There are three main ways your eyes can reflect the glory of God:

1. By what people see in you

2. By what you choose to see

3. By where you look

What Do People See in You?

Eyes tell a lot about a person. You can look into someone's eyes and discern a lot of things about them. Have you ever met someone who had no light in their eyes? I was listening to a band once, a very low-quality band, that was playing in Athens, Georgia (where I went to college). Because of their … ahem … lack of talent, I had a pretty good seat. I will never forget the eyes of the electric guitarist. They were deep and unfocused and downright scary. I kept trying to avoid them. To be honest, I was a little frightened of him.

A friend of mine was playing in the band as well. "Mike," I asked, "does that dude freak you out?" I figured Mike had practiced with him and was friends with him, so he had probably noticed the eyes before.

Being ever the optimist, Mike said, "He's such a nice guy,

Annie." As if I was being a jerk or something. *Hmph.* To which I replied that I thought he should look *right* into the guy's eyes. And when Mike did, he too was a bit freaked out. Because that dude had some *dark* eyes. Not just the color—I don't even remember the color. But they were dark and stormy and empty.

(Random moment: You won't even believe this, but literally, one of my contacts just fell out of my eye onto the keyboard. Okay, fine, y'all. I got the memo. Take out my contacts.)

God has something interesting to say about the look in someone's eyes, like that electric guitar player's.

Look at Matthew 6:22–23:

The eye is the lamp of the body. If your eyes are healthy, your whole body will be full of light. But if your eyes are unhealthy, your whole body will be full of darkness.

I love the way *The Message* paraphrases verse 22:

"Your eyes are windows into your body."

On nice evenings, I like to take a walk through my neighborhood right at dusk. Most people leave at least one shade open, and I can look in and see how their homes are decorated or who lives there. If the lights are on inside, I can see straight in. If not, I sigh and move on. I'm always excited, though, to see movement or people or an interesting piece of abstract art. The dark outside makes it easy to see the light in the homes. I love being able to see inside. I most especially enjoy these walks during the holiday season. The beauty of the lights twinkling on the Christmas trees, the wreaths on the doors, the electric candles in the windows—I just love being on the outside but being able to see what is going on inside. (Is that creepy? I hope not.)

The same goes for people. God made our eyes that way. In contrast to the darkness of our world, He wants people to be able to see into what's inside us—to experience His light and His love by looking into our eyes.

Peter Gabriel wrote a song called "In Your Eyes." Many Christian artists have done covers of it because it speaks so closely to this same idea. The chorus says,

> in your eyes, I am complete …
> in your eyes, the resolution of all the fruitless searches …
> in your eyes, oh, I want to be that complete

Really think about these words. Read them again. What else can nonbelievers have *except* fruitless searches? And the light in your eyes is that resolution—the end of their searching. People who don't know God want the light they see in your eyes. Don't ever forget that.

The line that sticks out to me the most? *"I want to be that complete."* Enough said. There is no light switch here. There is nothing you have "to do" to shine Jesus. Just loving Him and serving Him with the rest of your body brings that light to your eyes.

More than just thinking about what people see in your eyes, let's focus on what you choose to look at.

What Do You Choose to See?

As I said at the beginning of this chapter, glorifying God with our eyes is all about focusing. If you want a brief summary, here it is: We praise God with our eyes by choosing to focus on Him and the things He puts in front of us. When we focus on Him, when we look to Him, we are filled with light. Then people see that light. It's a chain reaction. A beautiful chain reaction.

It's also about choosing to see what's right in front of us. A moment ago, a dirty smell invaded my nostrils at the coffee shop I'm in right now. I looked up to see a middle-aged homeless man saunter into the building. He walked up to the line of patrons and, gripping two one-dollar bills in his hands, waited quietly for his turn. Around the room, eyes diverted. No one wanted to see him. Why?

He bought a canned drink and headed back out the door. No one, including myself, spoke to him, but everyone glanced. Noticed. But no one really saw.

I watched out the window as he left the shop. A girl just on the other side of the glass was sitting in the sunshine, reading her Bible. As the homeless man passed her, she watched him. I couldn't hear her, but I could tell she called out to him, and he turned around. She saw him. She may be the only one here who took that kind of time. He smiled as he listened to her. Then he turned and walked down the sidewalk.

Her eyes? They just glorified God. It didn't cost her anything except a moment. What did I do in that situation? Just kept typing. An opportunity to glorify God with my eyes was right before me and I ignored it. And my insides hurt because of it. She chose to see what God placed before her and responded to it. I didn't.

If we want to honor God with our eyes, we have to choose to see the hurt, the needs, the pain, and the bad that are in our world.

When I fell off my porch one day and sprained my ankle, I knew it was bad, but I didn't want to look at it. I could feel my shoe tightening and my sock stretching, and my ankle was warm to the touch. In my mind, it was black and blue and puffy. But I didn't want to see. Why? Because to see the bad makes it *real*. And, yes, when I finally got enough courage to actually look at the ankle, I headed straight to the emergency room, because that puppy was *huge*.

It's one thing to watch a commercial where a child is hungry. It's quite another to walk by a homeless family and see, right there before us, a child who is begging for food. It changes everything, doesn't it? The hard part of all this is that it's so sad to see. We don't want to look because we don't know what to do. But we have to look and then do something about it. (More about the "doing" part later.)

But there are also things that we, as women of God, have to choose not to see. Movies, television shows, magazine covers, websites, books—they are full of opportunities for us to fill our minds, by first filling our eyes, with evil. As a thirty-one-year-old, I still don't watch many R-rated movies. I don't want to fill my mind with that stuff, so I don't fill my eyes with that stuff.

What are your personal convictions about what is okay and not okay to see? Pray about it, because it's very important.

Where Do You Look?

My question is this: when things go wrong, where do you look? I love Psalm 121. In fact—and I'm not embarrassed to say this—I had a shirt that I wore all too often my tenth-grade year that had this scripture on it. I wore it with my purple hiking boots. Back off; I thought it was cool. I made it in the yearbook wearing that shirt. A proud moment.

Psalm 121:1–2 says,

> I lift up my eyes to the mountains—where does my help come from? My help comes from the LORD, the Maker of heaven and earth.

I didn't have an excellent adjustment period when I started college. In fact, in the spring of my freshman year, my feelings got hurt and it led to a complete breakdown. I lay on the couch and cried, I ate two cows worth of ice cream, and I cried some more. It was one of those moments when I had no idea how to deal with life, so I decided to go to a movie by myself. I told my roommates I would be back later, drove to the theater, and bought my ticket. I proudly purchased a large Diet Coke and a box of Sno-Caps. It felt so good and so independent. And it was painless, which was exactly what I was searching for. I wanted to make the pain go away, to pretend it didn't exist. Very unhealthy, people. Very unhealthy. (It's not unhealthy to go to a movie alone every now and again. It was just unhealthy to try to use that experience to smother the pain I was feeling.)

I thought it was very emo of me (though that wasn't a term back then). Now I know the truth: my heart was broken, and my eyes needed something to focus on. I was *looking* everywhere for something to help me stop hurting. I wanted to escape. I made the wrong choice. Exactly 105 minutes later and fifteen dollars poorer, I was right where I started. And probably a little dumber.

Psalm 121 gives us an answer for what to do with our pain, but not necessarily an easy one. Had I only turned my eyes to the Lord! My Help! Things would have gone so much smoother. And my heart would have healed quicker. It's true that it's easy to focus on other things than God when we're hurt. But Psalm 121 makes it clear: we need to look to Him for our healing.

Here's another song for you called "Turn Your Eyes upon Jesus" (we're really singin' today):

> *Turn your eyes upon Jesus,*
> *Look full in His wonderful face,*
> *And the things of earth will grow strangely dim*
> *In the light of His glory and grace.*

Have you ever seen a horse pulling a buggy? The horse has blinders on either side of its eyes. Horses, as you probably know, get spooked easily. So it's very important for horses to focus when they're around cars, buildings, teenagers, whatever, in order to keep the passengers safe. The buggy driver has placed those blinders on the horse for safety purposes. If the horse focuses on where it's going, it won't be distracted by the things around it, or scared by random, quick movements.

Look at Proverbs 4:25:

Let your eyes look straight ahead; fix your gaze directly before you.

Turn your eyes to Jesus. Put on blinders. Let the things of earth grow (and I love this word here) *strangely* dim. Not just ordinarily dim. But peculiarly dim. Abnormally dim. Surprisingly unimportant.

Look at Hebrews 12:1–2:

... Let us throw off everything that hinders and the sin that so easily entangles. And let us run with perseverance the race marked out for us, *fixing our eyes* on Jesus, the pioneer and perfecter of faith.... (emphasis mine).

We praise God by simply looking at Him. By fixing our eyes on Him. Because (remember) where our eyes are, our focus is as well. Make Him your focus. That's so easy to say, but what does it look like? I *despise* when people tell me stuff but really give me no direction.

So, here's some direction. Focusing on God means picking Him over other things. It means purposely spending time reading the Bible and actually trying to understand what it's saying. It means attempting to look at the world the way God does and see other people the way you *know* He sees them. It means turning your eyes away from things you know don't please Him or bring Him glory. Focusing on God is when you look to Him first and love Him the most.

Whew ... That's a lot to do. So let's finish up by looking one more place—at God's eyes. Because in the long run, this life really isn't about us; it's about Him. We act as a response to Him. I love what the Bible says about God's eyes.

Look at Psalm 34:15:

The eyes of the Lᴏʀᴅ are on the righteous, and his ears are attentive to their cry.

And Job 36:7:

[God] does not take his eyes off the righteous; he enthrones them with kings and exalts them forever.

So what is God's focus? What is it He is choosing to look at? You! The righteous one. The girl who goes after Him and tries to worship Him with her life. That's amazing to me. His eyes are focused on you.

Remember, we were created in His image. Just like our eyes draw our full attention somewhere, so do His. And that attention, my friend, is on *you*. I think that's beautiful.

In the end, here's the deal: just do whatever you know in your heart it takes to make God your focus, knowing that *you* are *His* focus. And your focus may not look like what everyone else is doing. God may ask you to quit watching something that everyone else seems to be watching. Or He may ask you to focus on something, like helping homeless people, that He's not asking anyone else to focus on. Make Him your main focus and then allow Him to move your eyes where He wants them.

I saw a picture recently that I loved—it was of a guy dressed in a khaki shirt and khaki shorts. He also had on hiking boots and he pretty much looked like the toughest guy you've ever met. He was sitting on top of a Jeep (instead of, you know, inside it!) as it flew through the Australian Outback. The caption on the bottom of the picture was this:

WHY BE CONVENTIONAL WHEN YOU CAN GET A BETTER VIEW?

Make choices that get you a better view of God. Even if it looks different from what the rest of the world does. No matter what it takes. Praise Him with your eyes.

chew on this

Ponder:

Look at Revelation 1:7

How does this verse relate to focus?

Who does it make you think of?

Read: Psalm 94:9; Psalm 123:1–2;

Look up: *eyes, see, blind, view*

Do it:

What is one way you can improve how you focus on God with your eyes?

What are your convictions about the types of movies, television shows, and other things you should (and shouldn't) be watching?

chapter 4

Ears

I have a soft spot in my heart for people who are hearing impaired. It's funny, isn't it, the people groups who move us? In my Bible study group last Tuesday morning, we talked about how God wired each human just differently enough that our hearts beat for different things. And for me, one group that always squeezes my heart is the deaf and hearing impaired.

I can't pinpoint when it began, but as far back as I can remember, I have honed in on those who are hearing impaired like they have a spotlight over their heads. In church. In restaurants. It's kinda crazy. Also, I can never resist watching the person doing sign language at any event. Even though I don't know what most of it means, I love seeing the art of it all. My dear friend Emily Freeman, author of *Grace for the Good Girl* and *Graceful*, is fluent in sign language, and it is one of my very favorite things about her. I love her for a lot of reasons, but I think I respect her so much because she has chosen to be a solution, a gift, to people who cannot hear. And her hands can move at warp speed—almost as fast as I can talk.

Almost.

When I coached high school soccer, my very favorite player was a deaf guy who was one of the finest goalies I've ever seen. He taught me all sorts of words in sign language, and I purchased, at a yard sale, a kids' book on sign language and read it daily to rehearse. He would laugh at me, because when I got to practice I would run up to him, fan my hands in his face to get his undivided attention, and then do a simple sign, like *boat*. He would say, "Good, Coach. A boat." Like I was a first grader or something.

I know. You're totally impressed. And yes, I still have the book from the yard sale. Those things can come in handy. You never know, people. (Is that what hoarders say? Uh oh.)

Sometimes I forget all the things I can hear. Maybe that is a ridiculous statement, but the more you pal around with the hearing-impaired community, the more you realize the tiniest things you hear can make a big difference.

Like a car horn honking.

Or someone saying your name across the room.

Or the sound of the washing machine finishing a load of towels and sheets. (I usually hate doing laundry, but I absolutely love folding sheets, so I'm kinda pumped about this load that's going right now.)

When I was in college, I went on a missions trip with a girl who was deaf. It was a fascinating experience for the rest of us, to watch and learn and she served and gave of herself, ministering to homeless people in California. The funniest moments were each night as all the girls laid down to go to sleep. (We were all sleeping on the floor of a church sanctuary. Classic missions trip memories, right?) Our deaf friend would always want to make sure all the jokes were done and the pillow talk had ceased before she took out her hearing aids. So over and over she would say, "You guys asleep? You guys? Hello? Okay—I'm turning off my ears. Don't have fun without me!"

Turning off her ears. I loved that. And we obeyed; that was kinda our cue to go to sleep. Which, as you know if you've been on a missions trip or a retreat or summer camp, teen girls—yes, even college girls—need to be told to go to bed.

Hear Me Out

Right now, think about all the things you can hear. I am listening to my laptop purr, my fingers click across the keyboard, and the soundtrack from *Pride and Prejudice* play softly from my computer. I can also hear that my neighbor has just pulled into the driveway, and that the heater just kicked in—hallelujah! I can hear some random cat that patrols our neighborhood scurry across my front porch. (Why does this cat insist on coming onto my porch? Grrrr …) But without my ears, without the ability to hear, I would be missing so many things that are going on around me.

I love hearing. One of my favorite things is hearing people call my name. In fact, and let's put this in the category of things we keep just between us girls, a deciding factor when I have a crush on a dude is what it sounds like when he says my name. I had a crush in college named Jim, and I promise you the *only* thing I liked about him was that he said my name really well—he's from *south* Georgia, so it came out slow and long and deep, kind of like "Ainnn-eee." And oh my biscuits, I wanted to marry that man (except that there was no other thing I even remotely enjoyed about him). The crush fizzled.

I love to hear little boys laugh, and I love to hear popcorn popping. I love to hear my friends tell a great story, or a heart-breaking one. I love to listen to people worship, and I love to listen to a creek as the water rolls over stones on the bottom.

But I'll have to admit that there is one thing I love most about my ears: they don't get me in nearly as much trouble as my mouth does. See, your ears only take in information—they are unable to give out information. Yes, you can hear something you aren't supposed to, but that's about as far as it goes. (Unless you tell what you've heard … which isn't your ears' fault, now is it?) Your ears don't have the power that your tongue has to ruin your day, your friendships, or your life. Your ears don't have the strength to effect change the way your hands do. Your ears, along with your eyes, are a main source of intake in your life.

Don't be mistaken—this doesn't diminish the importance of your ears or the ability of your ears to be instruments of righteousness. Your ears are still a vital part of your body—and a part that you can use to glorify God.

Think about this quote from Judy Garland (better known as Dorothy in *The Wizard of Oz*): "For it was not into my ear you whispered, but into my heart."

Voltaire, a famous French philosopher, had a similar thought: "The ear is the avenue to the heart."

Music is one of the powerful ways the ears affect the heart. I love listening to really good music. Living in Nashville, Tennessee, I often have the opportunity to hear musicians live. Many times the best shows feature musicians I've never heard of but end up enjoying immensely. The interesting thing about music is that it doesn't stop with our ears. When it comes into our ears, it then moves to our minds and then into our hearts. At least, that's how it works for me.

Some of my current faves, you ask? Dave Barnes, Matt Wertz, Andrew Peterson, Brooke Fraser, and Ellie Holcomb. Those five are constantly in a rotational fight on my iPod. I'll be honest, sometimes it gets ugly in there.

Have you ever seen someone close his or her eyes while listening to music? I watched one night as my friend's dad sat in a chair, eyes closed, and sang along with the Christmas carols playing through the speakers in the house. The music was doing far more than simply passing through his ears. It was reminding him, moving him, calming him—all sorts of things that the power of music is capable of doing.

Has anyone ever said something to you and then asked you to forget it? Or have you ever seen a court case where the judge says, "I would like the jury to disregard that last comment and not consider it in determining guilt or innocence"? Yeah, right!

It's impossible. Because what comes into your ears, for the most part, stays in your mind. And sometimes in your heart.

Look at Job 13:1:

My eyes have seen all this, my ears have heard and understood it.

So not only do famous people like Judy Garland see that the ears have a direct connection to the heart, apparently folks in the Bible think the same thing. The ears take in the information, test it, and understand it. What goes into your ears fills your mind. What you hear influences who you are. If you want to be a person of praise, full of good things, you need to hear what that verse says.

When I was in college, I listened to a variety of music. Some was good, some of it wasn't. Most of the songs I enjoyed were fine, but a few (truthfully, a few of my favorites) had more than one cuss word in them. Though listening to the edited versions was an option, the unedited songs were the ones on my computer. I thought it was no big deal to listen to them once in a while … or once in a week … or once in a day.

My roommates and I sat down to dinner one night in our apartment. I honestly don't even remember what we were talking about, but all of a sudden, when I went to say something, I said the f-word. The big one. Whoa. They stopped talking or eating and stared at me. Then they turned pale, and their eyes bugged out. But so did mine. I couldn't believe it! I had never intended to say that—it just came out. Needless to say, I jumped out of my chair, ran to my room, and deleted that music immediately. Seriously. I did. I knew the moment that word came out of my mouth exactly which song had put it in my head. After deleting the song, I returned to the table and continued to eat the hamburger and sweet-potato fries we had made.

(By the way, do you know how to make sweet-potato fries? Because they are *super* easy and *super* delicious. Just look in the appendix for the recipe.)

Back to the music (though you are really going to love that recipe) … I wasn't praising God with my ears when I was listening to those songs. I was allowing all sorts of rubbish in, and you know the old saying that we all hate—trash in, trash out. And I lived it. Trash came pouring out all over my roommates' dinners.

Truthfully, whether you want to acknowledge it or not, this doesn't just apply to music. This applies to anything you listen to—music, television, movies, or your friends. And I tell you all this simply to remind you of this fact: what you put in your ears goes into your heart. You can act like you aren't affected by the things you hear, but I'm sorry to say you are. We all are. It's part of our makeup and humanness.

Those words I heard, and repeated at the dinner table, were in my heart. And they came out of my mouth. As always, this is a personal conviction thing. I'm not setting a standard for you; nor should you set a standard for anyone else. I'm not telling you that if you aren't dialed into the local Christian radio station, you're going to bust out a cuss word at any moment. I would be lying if I said I listened to worship music all the time. I do listen to it a good bit, but there is other good music out there that won't include questionable themes or lyrics. (Check out the musicians listed in the appendix.)

I'm not your boss or your mama, but I am saying that you need to ask the Lord what He requires of you. And remember, it's not just music. It's movies, television shows, and conversations. What does it look like, for you, to praise God with your ears? I don't like talking about the "do nots" of life, but sometimes we have to. We need to hold ourselves to a higher standard than the world, and that's not just what comes out of us, but what goes into us as well.

Listen Up

On the other hand, there are definite things we *can* do to glorify God with our ears. First of all, the obvious answer is we should listen to the Lord. He has plans for us that are so good (Jeremiah 29:11), but we have to choose to listen to them. I get nervous when people talk about "hearing God," because a lot of times I feel like I can't do that. I sit there, dead silent, with my eyes squinted shut as tight as I make them. I try to calm my mind and focus just on God. And I hear *nothing*. It's frustrating and annoying and discouraging. Then I'm over it ... quickly. But then I saw this verse, and it's changed how I listen:

> He wakens me morning by morning, *wakens my ear* to listen like one being instructed.
>
> Isaiah 50:4, emphasis mine

Choose to glorify the Lord by listening to Him and asking

Him each morning to waken your ears to His voice. Take time to grow this discipline. No, it isn't always fun or easy. But most things aren't, if we want to be really honest. Practice listening to God. And remember, the Lord can speak to you in *many* different ways—through His Word, through other people like mentors and pastors, through your heart. Just listen. He wants to talk to you. He gave you ears to hear Him. So when you pray about hearing Him, ask Him to waken your ears. Pray Isaiah 50:4.

And remember that you are never too young or too old or too cute or too dumb to hear the Lord. If you've been a Christian since you were two, or if you've been a Christian for two minutes, God can and will talk to you. Just ask Him, then listen.

Do You Hear What I Hear?

Remember in Matthew 25:40 where Jesus said, "Whatever you [do] for the least of these … you [do] for me"? When it comes to our ears, I think this lesson is an important one. Because in addition to listening to God, the other main way we glorify God with our ears is by listening to others.

There are three main things we hear:

1. What people say *around* us

2. What people say *about* us

3. What people say *to* us

What People Say Around Us

First, it's important to be attentive to what people say *around us*. We need to be paying enough attention to our surroundings that we hear when people are in need or hurting, and can reach out to them with God's love. A lonely classmate probably won't come out and say they're hurting, but you may overhear her saying something that keys you in. You may hear a crowd of people picking on someone. Suddenly you have the opportunity to defend that person, and it's all because you are listening to what was being said around you.

My friend Dawn decided that while she was babysitting recently, she would take the kids to get burritos for lunch. (Aren't babysitting field trips the best? Makes time fly, huh?) As Dawn got the five kids out of the car, she heard a woman screaming. The lady wasn't hurt, but she was yelling at a man standing by his car. And she was using words that would have given that parking lot an R-rating. The man had apparently asked the woman to close her door or something, and it had caused her to fly off the handle. Dawn, unbuckling the little ones from their seats, noticed the older kids staring at the woman with eyes as big as saucers. Dawn had to protect those poor ears.

"Ma'am!" she yelled at the top of her lungs. "Please stop until I can get these kids inside!" The lady, almost as if coming out of a daze, looked at Dawn, looked at the kids, and then got into her car. Dawn wasn't ugly to the woman, but the woman was probably embarrassed for acting so crazy in a public place. It was important that Dawn pay attention to what was being said *around* her. She protected the kids' ears and might have saved that man from a thirty-minute confrontation. And she might have saved that woman from going to jail.

What People Say About Us

Second, we often hear what people say *about* us. I think this is true more than we want to admit. But we don't have to believe everything we hear.

Look at Job 12:11:

Does not the ear test words as the tongue tastes food?

Believe this verse. Test everything you hear about yourself, or anyone else, for that matter. Remember, not everything is true. People say things for a million different reasons, over half of them probably with the intention of hurting someone else. So when you hear something that is said about you, hold it up to the truth. If it matches, keep it. If it doesn't, trash it.

An acquaintance said some really ugly stuff about me one time. And I mean *really* nasty and *really* specific stuff. Kind of like, "Wow, you must know *way* more about me than I thought you did to be able to be *this* mean." Yeah, it wasn't fun. And when it was over, she had said about fifteen different things about me that in my deep hurt, I couldn't even determine if they were true or false. I hoped they were false, but I didn't know.

So I called up my best friends, Molly and Haley, and we went to get pizza. While sitting at the table, I pulled out the list of things that this girl had said about me. "Which of these are true?" I asked. "Because I don't know." The three of us went through the list statement by statement, and they were honest with me about what they did and didn't agree with.

So whether people are saying ugly stuff about you, or being way complimentary, compare it to the truth. I trust my best friends completely and I trust their knowledge of God's truth for me, so I knew they could help me out. That's real-life accountability. To glorify God is to take what people say about you, hold it up to the light of the truth of God's Word and to people that you trust, and only hang on to the things that will make you more like Jesus.

What People Say to Us

Third, we can glorify God by listening to what people say *to us*. One of the truest statements I've ever heard is this: people always hear but don't always listen. Pay attention to your friends and the things they are saying to you. Listen to your parents, teachers, and pastors. You can hear everything; choose to listen.

We're so quick to interchange these two words, I think it might be good to see the differences in the definitions of "hear" and "listen":

- Hear—to receive information by the ear

- Listen—to give attention with the ear

Interesting, huh? The main differences I see in these definitions is this: Hearing involves no activity or effort from us; listening does. We "receive" when we hear; we "give" when we listen. Think about that. You have to give something to listen, make a sacrifice, even if it's just a few seconds of time. Ernest Hemingway said it better than I can: "When people talk, listen completely. Most people never listen."

What if a friend is trying to tell you about her broken heart? What if your little brother is telling you about his first baseball game? What if your mother is telling you about her junior year in high school? All of it is easy to hear; not all of it is fun to listen to. But remember that how you are treating these people is how you are treating the Lord. You're representing Him to a hurting world—so praise Him by loving and truly listening to the people in your world. "Listen completely," as Hemingway said.

I found a statistic that says that more than two hundred thousand Americans are deaf, and three million have serious hearing problems. I wonder what the survey would say about how many people are deaf to *God's* voice? Or how many millions of people around the world have a *listening* problem? Let's not be counted among those. Let's be known for glorifying God with our ears.

chew on this

Ponder:

We are made in God's image.

We have ears to hear. God has ears to hear.

What we hear goes into our hearts. What He hears goes into His heart.

So ... How does that make you feel about prayer?

Read: Nehemiah 1:6; Psalm 34:15; ; Psalm 94:9; Isaiah 59:1

Look up: *hear, listen, ears*

Do it:

What is one thing you can work on or do this week to glorify God with your ears?

chapter 5

Mouth

"**Okay, so I saw them together** at the mall, but really, I don't *know* that they're dating. I'm just saying …"

"Promiscuous girl, you're teasing me. You know what I want, and I got what you need …"

"Come, Lord Jesus, come … Come, Lord Jesus, come …"

"I could not believe it when I heard what he got arrested for. I mean, I could have guessed he was into that stuff, because this one time …"

"You are my strength when I am weak; You are the treasure that I seek …"

"I just heard that was happening last night …"

"I'm praying for you, friend. Let me know if I can do anything for you."

"No, I don't think she's the kind of friend you need. Did you hear what she did last year after prom? I shouldn't be telling you this, but …"

"I'm only telling you this because I think it's something you should definitely pray about. See, she was talking to him on the phone when …"

"Praise God from whom all blessings flow …"

Whew. Talk about saltwater and freshwater flowing from the same spring (see James 3)! I don't know about you, but that makes me feel sick to my stomach. I guess because at one point in my life or another, I've said all of these things. Of course, probably not back-to-back like this, but all from the same mouth. If I was cool enough to have a stenographer (like the lady who types what is said in court) follow me around, all these things would be somewhere on her transcript. Even as an adult, I still struggle with controlling my mouth at times and making sure that the words flowing from it are life-giving.

"We all talk about other people, Annie. It's just a part of our lives. I mean, let's be real. Some stuff just needs to be talked about. If she didn't want us to talk about that, she shouldn't have done it, right?"

Wrong!

It's very interesting to me how my everyday life and writing work together. This is somewhat off topic, but follow this rabbit trail and I'll bring you back around. See, as I planned out the chapter on glorifying God with your mouth, I never asked God to make me live it. Apparently, this isn't one of those "He needs permission" kind of things. (What is, really?) Instead, He just gave me a day to watch and hurt and experience the pain and joy that mouths can cause.

Today is Sunday. I got up and went to church this morning and sang my heart out to God. I saw some friends I adore, and they spoke kind words about my cute green shirt. (And listen, it is so cute. I love it.) They asked about my job, how things are in my life, and if I've met any interesting fellows lately. Their words were encouraging and uplifting. I returned the encouragement, asked about a new house that was just completed, and inquired after a mother's health. I told some high school students how glad I was to see them and how much I love them. Then I played with some kids in our church and laughed, rather loudly, as they jumped off the plastic chairs in our church building. Afterward, a group of us went to lunch at a local pizza restaurant, and I ate salad and a slice of Florentine pizza, which is so good. Do you ever get to eat that kind of pizza? It has artichoke hearts, spinach, tomatoes, grilled chicken, and feta. Gracious, it's delicious. I had one happy mouth. So far, so good, right?

Then a friend of mine mentioned something she heard about me. Pure gossip, not truth, about a boy and a nonexistent crush, and I was mad. Some kid running his mouth just dropped a gossip grenade on my day. I ended up spending honestly two hours resolving the situation that this one comment, made about me, caused. Whether intended to hurt me or not, it did, and honestly, it still does. My mouth didn't do anything wrong here, but I'm paying the price.

Then my sister called from Africa to ask about what someone else said about her at church this very morning. How she heard so quickly (I'm talking four hours later), I'll never know. I rolled my eyes and answered. Did she seriously just spend a billion dollars to hear gossip about herself?

Could this conversation not have occurred over email?

Literally five minutes later, I got a call from a friend, who explained to me that apparently I have been accused of dropping my own gossip grenade, and other people are mad. Huh? Probably for once in my life, I really didn't say what reportedly came out of my mouth. And so I spent another two hours trying to clean up *that* shrapnel.

Now what are the chances that all of this would take place in one day? Is this some sort of nightmare? Or is it a weird movie, like *The Truman Show*? What is the likelihood that my mouth, and other mouths, would be involved in so many different circumstances—good and bad? Why did this happen? I hope that I'm living it, and living to tell you about it, so you won't have to experience this.

Our mouths are so powerful. (End of rabbit trail—see, we came back around, didn't we?) Just look how in one day, in twelve hours exactly, mouths have changed everything. Something as small as a tongue has rocked my life. Look how other people's mouths affected me. Drastically. Sorrowfully. Whether involving me or someone I care about, people have talked, and I have been hurt. Deeply. And disturbed.

I'm disturbed because these mouths that are talking are my friends from church. The people I'm accused of talking about are my friends from church. These aren't worldly heathens who could just use a little Jesus and it would straighten them all out; these are people I trust with my heart and spiritual life and depend on in a crisis. These are people I have prayed for, prayed with, and lived with, through thick and thin.

But our mouths have betrayed our hearts. Maybe we don't trust each other, or dare I say love each other, the way we thought we did. I don't feel loved or trusted the way I did yesterday. All because of words. Including, apparently, my own.

The Bible makes it plain and simple in Matthew 12:34:

For the mouth speaks what the heart is full of.

Read that again. Please. What comes out of your mouth is what is already in your heart. As we've talked about already when we discussed ears, trash in equals trash out. And that is all there is to it. So I know better how the people talking about me *feel* about me—I know what is in their hearts toward me. And the part that hurts the most is that the people who thought I was talking about them *think* that's my heart toward them. Have mercy.

Forgive us, Lord, when we don't honor You with our mouths. I am grieved, God, over my behavior, my friends' behavior, and the looseness of our tongues. Call us to a higher standard. May we be people who praise You with our mouths.

The Tongue Unplugged

Somehow, in the modern-girl psyche, there is this belief or thought that if you tell someone all the secrets you know, that makes the two of you best friends. So instead of keeping the confidences I've promised, I just tell *one* person, because after all, she is my "best friend" ... and that *one* person may tell *two* people. Within a matter of days, the secret that only I knew is all over the school or church or Internet. And what I thought was building a really strong friendship has actually just proved that I can't keep my mouth shut. This is hard for me, because I feel like I have forty-five best friends, and if one of them tells me something, surely it's okay for all of the other best friends to know. But that isn't the case, and I've learned over and over again (I wish it only took once) that it takes lots of work to be trusted and only one mistake to lose that trust.

Ouch, huh? Trust me, sister, I've been there. It is not fun. I've gotten a whole lot better at keeping my mouth shut, but it was about ten years too late to save some friendships. Once you are considered untrustworthy, there's really no way to recover that trust without a lot of work.

So, obviously, we can see how *not* to praise God with our mouths. And yes, you are welcome for those real-life examples that have officially ruined an otherwise lovely Sunday. Truthfully, everyone knows not to gossip—it isn't something you sit there and ponder over whether it's a good idea. You know it's not.

Liar, Liar

Another mouth issue I dealt with a lot as I was growing up was lying. Somewhere in the back of my mind, I was convinced that it was better to make up a story and have everyone happy than tell the truth and make someone mad. So that's what I did. *For years.* It's still pretty embarrassing to think about some of the whoppers I told, and the temptation to lie is still something I fight in my mind. I desperately dislike the feeling of disappointing someone I love or hurting people's feelings, so my first inclination is to say the "right thing," even if it's a lie. Most of the time, my mind and heart work together to send the truth out of my mouth. But when I was a younger woman, and as kid, that wasn't the case. Lying is based solely and completely on insecurities, and as you know about me already, my mind was filled with lies and insecurities, so that was also what overflowed.

I don't like to talk about that part of my life very much because it's really shameful to me. Even seeing old friends from elementary school makes me cringe to this day. Because I know how they see me—as a liar. As someone who never told the truth. And that's a hard stigma to break, especially if you aren't really friends anymore.

Luckily, I've held on to some of those friendships, mainly two girls I've known since elementary school. Danielle and Jennifer survived a lot of my fictional stories and have lived to tell about them. In fact, I'm pretty sure they *love* to tell about them, because the stories are so ridiculous. I think Danielle would say her personal favorite was in middle school, when I told an elaborate story about seeing an angel and a demon in my bedroom. The sad part is I don't remember even telling that lie, but they both remember it and love to bring it up as possibly the most ridiculous thing I said. *Ever.*

I tell you all of this, even though it embarrasses me, because I need you to hear the truth that my mouth hasn't always been a friend to me, and oftentimes it has been the absolute downfall of my friendships and myself. Now that I'm older, I've grown in my relationship with the Lord and in my confidence of who I am in Him, and this is rarely, if ever, a struggle anymore. I may feel the pressure to exaggerate a story or want to say the "right thing," but the truth wins now. Sadly, I can't go back and erase the lies that riddled my childhood.

Before we move on, without too much drama, let's just list some other ways we're inclined to use our mouths incorrectly:

- cussing
- screaming at someone (in a non-cheering kind of way)
- boasting or bragging
- using sarcasm (don't even get me started on this one …)
- gossiping (did we cover this one sufficiently?)
- singing crude lyrics
- telling crude or rude jokes
- making racist comments
- complaining
- being disrespectful (or, as my mama calls it, "talkin' back")

I could write a chapter on each of these things. That just shows how surprisingly powerful our mouths can be. Let the Lord highlight the areas that apply to you. Only you go everywhere with yourself (make sense?), so only you know everything you say, and the areas you need His light to shine on. I have found that the best way to deal with this stuff is to literally pray, "Lord, make me sensitive to honoring You with my mouth." And He will.

I talk a lot. I just do. It's part of my makeup. And for a long time, I was really sarcastic. It's an easy laugh and a quick reply, and it makes you look cool, so I was all over it. But when I was in college, other people's sarcasm began to hurt my feelings. As I talked with my friend Hannah about it, she said, "I'm really surprised to hear how much this bothers you. You are *way* more sarcastic than those people." Yikes. Not cool. So starting that day, I asked God to make me really sensitive to my own sarcasm—to stop me in my tracks when I was getting ready to say something hurtful, even if it was unintentional and just meant for a laugh. Since then, I can hardly make a sarcastic comment without feeling like I've been punched in the gut. Not to say I haven't been sarcastic, but when I choose to say the zinger, even though I probably shouldn't, I feel terrible.

And I'm glad I do. That's conviction. That's God stepping into my situation, through the Holy Spirit, and showing me how to live well for His glory. Then maybe next time the chance arises to be sarcastic, I'll stop *before* I say something cutting, instead of after.

(Should I be embarrassed at how many personal examples I have for this chapter? Sheesh!)

Read James 3 first from whatever version of the Bible you use. Then read verses 3–12 from *The Message*. (I like how easy this version is to read and how simple it is to apply to this issue. If you don't own a copy of *The Message*, you can go online to biblegateway.com.)

A bit in the mouth of a horse controls the whole horse. A small rudder on a huge ship in the hands of a skilled captain sets a course in the face of the strongest winds. A word out of your mouth may seem of no account, but it can accomplish nearly anything—or destroy it!

It only takes a spark, remember, to set off a forest fire. A careless or wrongly placed word out of your mouth can do that. By our speech we can ruin the world, turn harmony to chaos, throw mud on a reputation, send the whole world up in smoke and go up in smoke with it, smoke right from the pit of hell.

This is scary: You can tame a tiger, but you can't tame a tongue—it's never been done. The tongue runs wild, a wanton killer. With our tongues we bless God our Father; with the same tongues we curse the very men and women he made in his image. Curses and blessings out of the same mouth!

My friends, this can't go on. A spring doesn't gush fresh water one day and brackish the next, does it? Apple trees don't bear strawberries, do they? Raspberry bushes don't bear apples, do they? You're not going to dip into a polluted mud hole and get a cup of clear, cool water, are you?

When I read scriptures like this, I'm reminded that our heavenly Father is the all-time greatest Author. Words so true have never been spoken, nor will they be spoken as eloquently as the Lord spoke them here through James, the brother of Jesus. The power of the tongue is undeniable. So whom are you empowering? How are you using this mighty instrument? In the end, it all boils down to this: When you open your mouth, whom are you praising?

That's mildly frightening to you, isn't it? To me too. Because there are only two choices. Well, three, I guess. You are either praising God, yourself, or ... well, the Enemy. Gossip has given the Devil praise because he has been able to temporarily destroy what God has built. Again, my heart is broken over my sin—past, present, and unfortunately, future.

The real question is this: What does it look like to honor God with your mouth? What would it look like to live a life of praise with your mouth? The good news is that, just like our friends in *Star Wars*, this force can be used for good as well as evil.

The Power to Make

With our mouths, we are constantly creating. And we have that gift because we're made in God's image. He is the Creator. I love the novel *The Magician's Nephew* by C. S. Lewis. Chronologically, it comes before *The Lion, the Witch, and the Wardrobe*. In it, the reader gets to experience the creation of Narnia. When the characters arrive there, it is nothing but a black, empty place. All they know is that their feet are on a solid surface. Then suddenly stars begin to shine and the sun rises, plants and trees begin to grow, and animals are birthed out of mounds in the ground. This is all being done by one beautiful voice. And that is the voice of the lion, Aslan (who is the representation of God). He sings, and the world is created. With each change in His voice, a different part of the world is made, and the characters are amazed.[1] I think I would be too.

God creates with His words. Read the first two chapters of Genesis, and you'll see proof. And because we are made in God's image, we have the opportunity to do what He does. We can create. We don't have the amount of power God has (obviously), but He made our tongues so that they possess the power to create. Praising God with our mouths is about creating good things with the words we speak, or write.

I thought about this yesterday as I sat at a dear friend's wedding. The bride and groom spoke a commitment—and suddenly, just with words, their lives were tied together until death separates them. The beauty of those words, the strength in them, caused me to pause. I thought about how carelessly I throw words around, just like it says in James 3, and yet how powerful they can be.

With words of gossip, chaos and sadness are created.

With words of loving encouragement, life and blessing arise.

With words of hatred, a bitter heart and brokenness are birthed.

With words of praise, a happy heart is encouraged.

With words of biting sarcasm, embarrassment and fear are given authority.

---

1. If you want to read the scene for yourself, see C. S. Lewis, *The Magician's Nephew* (New York, Macmillan, 1970), pages 98–116.

With your tongue, you create.

The question you can ask yourself daily is this: *What am I creating with the words I am saying?*

Don't be deceived. Though your tongue is strong, it is *not* more powerful than the God who created it. The Holy Spirit is your Restrainer, your muzzle, if you don't mind me saying so. Or, if you're shy, the Holy Spirit can be the force that releases your tongue to speak. With as much as I talk, it's a constant prayer of mine that the Lord would guide my tongue and use it to glorify Him. That He would constantly be my Muzzle. Does that always happen? No. (But not because of Him; because of me.)

Look at Proverbs 10:19:

> When words are many, sin is not absent, but he who holds
> his tongue is wise (NIV 1984).

Yikes. I know that all too well. But, please, don't live in fear of what will come out of your mouth. That isn't the point. Instead, constantly check yourself, asking yourself if what you are about to say is going to bring glory to God. If it will bring glory to yourself or anything else, keep it in. Hold your tongue. Make a choice.

And like I said, the same goes for shy people. You have nothing to be afraid of, my friend. Use the voice that God has given you and pray the same prayer—that God would be glorified in your words, though they may be few. Seek and find your confidence in Him.

Love others with the words you say. Train your tongue to be an instrument of righteousness. You have no idea the good that can come from one well-spoken word. Or do you? Have you ever been on the receiving end of a quick comment that changed everything?

I went to visit my grandmother in her nursing home last week. She has been sick for a while and isn't always coherent. But, in God's goodness, she was almost completely normal on this particular visit. She spoke something to my heart that I won't soon forget. Let me tell you that nothing soothes like kind words from a grandmother, especially one who is far away, physically or mentally. It was just five words, "And I think it's time …," but the Lord used those words powerfully in my heart and life. She doesn't even remember saying them. But her kind words stuck to my heart.

Look at Proverbs 16:24:

> Gracious words are a honeycomb, sweet to the soul and healing to the bones.

Living in a new town, I find it makes all the difference in the world when friends say uplifting things to me. After a wedding last night, my friend Rachael stopped me and said, "My life here is better because you are in it." It took her fifteen seconds to say those words, but I'm pretty sure they made the kind of impact on my heart that will last for years and years.

Work at this one, girls. May you be known for the blessings that are created by your words. My prayer for you is that lives would be changed, hearts would be healed, and souls would be touched by the pleasant words you share.

Change a life, and glorify God, with just a word.

chew on this

Ponder:

What is your greatest strength when it comes to the words you say?

Are you an encourager? A great friend? A calming voice? A good listener (i.e., you keep your mouth shut)?

What is your greatest weakness? Gossip? Lying? Cussing?

How are your greatest strengths and weaknesses related?

Do you see any places where your greatest strength and your greatest weakness are similar?

Read: James 3

Look up: *tongue, mouth, words, speak*

Do it:

Listen to yourself today. What are you talking about? How is it honoring God?

chapter 6

Shoulders

Call me crazy, but I used to love to wrestle. It started with my dad; my sister and I were in elementary school, and we would attack him out of nowhere. He would toss us around like sacks of flour. I mean, I assume we looked like sacks of flour. To be honest, I've never really seen a sack of flour, nor have I seen a sack of flour being tossed anywhere. So that entire analogy just fell apart. But you know what I meant.

As I grew older, I still loved to wrestle around. More than a fighter, I think you would have called me an instigator. I'd get near my friend John and just punch him in the arm. He'd say, "Don't mess with me, Annie," and usually that would only cause me to want to make more trouble. So I'd poke and punch and mess around enough to get my friends all riled up, and then they would attack.

I usually got thrown around, tackled, knocked down, and covered in a plethora of bumps and bruises. Yet I totally loved it. There was something ridiculously hilarious about the whole thing. It was like having the big brothers I had always wanted—beatings included.

One wrestling incident in college will forever remain in my memory.

(But before I tell you this story, let me say that I don't think this was a good idea. Anymore. At the time I loved it. Now, I think it's a pretty poor use of free time and friendships. Just consider that my preface.)

A bunch of us who volunteered with the youth group were hanging out at the youth minister's house. Two of the dudes who worked with the youth group had played football in high school. And they weren't built like kickers—they were the offensive linemen. *Big.* I mean, 270 pounds kind of big. And even though they didn't play football anymore, they had managed to maintain their hugeness.

So I, being hilarious and looking to cause a fight, started messing with both of them. Mark and John were swatting at me like a fly. "Get outta here," Mark said. "You know I'll beat you until you cry." Well, that was my cue to start acting like a fool. And I did. Next thing I knew, they were shoving me back and forth, pinning me to the floor, and pretty much scrubbing my face into the carpet.

While John held me facedown, knee in my back, Mark began to pull at my arms. Of course, I was trying to toss and turn and escape from this, but there was no hope. I was trapped.

I mean, their combined body weight was like wrestling with a lion. And I don't know what you've heard about me, but I'm actually *not* stronger than a lion.

Then Mark decided to actually sit on my back. And while I was fighting as much as I could, I heard him say, "Who wants to go on a boat ride?" I knew I was in big trouble. Mark pulled my arms up and began to row them like they were oars on a boat. And the crowd went wild—all our friends who were there thought it was so very funny.

Until something tore in my shoulder. I didn't know what happened; I just knew that we *all* heard the sound, like paper ripping. And my right arm dropped with a thud to the carpet. Both the boys jumped up, and looks of horror mixed with concern crossed their faces at the same time. I tried to shake it off. I always wanted to look tough, and I never wanted to look like I was getting beat. But there wasn't much I could do. Everyone had heard the sound, and I knew I was in bad shape. My arm would move, but not without a lot of pain. I didn't cry, thank you very much, but I hurt. Bad.

That week I went to the doctor, and sure enough, I had a tear in my rotator cuff, the group of muscles at the top of my shoulder. Though I can wear just about any accessory with some sass, it's hard to find things that go well with a grey-and-white sling, which I ended up having to wear for a month. I couldn't lift anything. I couldn't wash my hair. I couldn't even wear a backpack. I struggled to do the simplest things. My elbow, fingers, hand, and arm weren't even affected. But because my shoulder was injured, everything was broken.

Horrible, right? Needless to say, that was my last wrestling match. Annie–0, Lion–1. And that's how the score remains to this day.

A Shoulder is a Terrible Thing to Waste

As I sit and write at this coffee shop, my favorite barista is wearing a sling. Tim is his name. He's a hard worker and super friendly. One time he made my drink wrong. I ordered a chai cider, which is supposed to be three parts apple cider, one part chai. He did it the other way around, and to be honest, it was gross. But I was choking it down because he's just such a nice guy that I didn't want to hurt his feelings (I have issues). About two minutes later, he comes up and brings me a new drink, apologizing for making the first one wrong. Nice guy.

A minute ago, Tim walked by my table in the sling, so I stopped him and asked what had happened. (Did I mention I'm extremely nosy? Because I am. What makes me think it's my business to ask him what happened? I have no idea. But I did.)

And sure enough, it's a shoulder injury. Playing football on Thanksgiving Day, Tim managed to stretch the tendons and muscles in his shoulder. He said he should only be in the sling for ten to fourteen days, but when you're trying to make a white-chocolate mocha and deliver a chicken-salad sandwich simultaneously to a customer, two weeks is a long time. (That sentence just made my mouth water.)

Wow. So far every story I've told is a shoulder disaster. That can't be encouraging you to celebrate your shoulders. Sorry about that. Let's talk nice about our shoulders now.

It's obvious your shoulders are important to you as a human and a mammal who walks upright. (You do walk upright, correct? Because if you walk on all fours, I'm going to assume you're an animal who can read. If you are an animal who can read, let's talk. I think we could be making some money.) Your shoulders literally keep your arms connected to your body. Duh. But in a spiritual sense, in the sense of what shoulders represent, there is so much more. When I think about you and who you are becoming, I think about how important your shoulders are going to be as you mature.

Stand Tall, Sista

You know, your body *learns* how to stand—you aren't born with this ability. Standing with posture is one of the first focuses in ballet class. Please tell me you were forced to take at least one ballet class. I used to bawl my eyes out as I struggled to put on those dumb pink tights. I hated them. I hated ballet. But Mama made me go because the teachers work on your posture. I learned to point my toes and stand with my shoulders back.

Standing up tall and having good posture is a sign of confidence and elegance. Your shoulders should be held back and pushed down for you to look more ladylike. It's better for the health of your back. And it's better for your heart. For your soul. For your inner sista.

Try something. Go to a long mirror or walk to the mirror above the sink in the bathroom. (Uh, take this book with you so you can read the next instructions, 'cause I think you're going to really miss the illustration if you are running from room to room to read the next sentence.) Stand in front of the mirror, hunch over, and cross your arms. Notice how closed off you look. Do you see that it looks like you're hiding? Hiding your heart? What is your face doing? What are some words that come to mind when you see yourself like this? Maybe jot those down in the margins of this book.

Now stand tall. Push your shoulders back and down, uncross your arms, and open up your chest. What's different about your face? About your stance? About how you feel? Write that down as well.

In fact, Moodraiser.com says that experimenting with your posture is the number three way to raise your mood. (Reading over the list, I'm fairly convinced that it was written by a dude, because ice cream doesn't even make the top ten. Oh, the shame.) How funny that how you stand completely affects how you feel. It is obvious that looking up and facing the world is far better for you than looking down.

Glorifying God with your body, making your shoulders instruments of righteousness, means walking proudly and confidently. Push those shoulders back, open up your chest, and hold your head high. You are a great girl, and the world deserves to know that. You are loved by a big God, and He knows all about you. Need a reminder? Go back to the "All of You" chapter and read those verses again. They are true for you.

When you let the world know you, people will get a glimpse of Jesus. And the only time they will feel comfortable enough to get to know you is when you look approachable and available.

So stand tall. Use those shoulders to show the world that you, my friend, are proud to be you.

Hunker Down, Hairy Dawg

Let me first say that no, I am not calling you a dog. And I am definitely not calling you hairy. I went to the University of Georgia, and this is one of the cheers—"Hunker down, hairy dog! Hunker down for a fight!" Just in case this phrase is totally foreign to you, to *hunker down* is to "assume a defensive position to resist difficulties." So when the tough times come (and sad to say, they always do), you just hang on, put your shoulders forward like you're going to tackle somebody, and ride them out.

I think because this is a football cheer, I picture a football player in my head—bent over, in the ready position, knowing that a hit is coming. Not *thinking* he may get hit, not wondering if a hit is coming, but positioning himself in a way that says, "Bring it on! I'm strong enough to take this." His shoulders are forward, one hand resting on the ground, ready to go.

And that's what we have to do in real life too. Put our shoulders down and take the hits as they come. But what does that look like? It looks like choosing God even when it's hard; loving people even when you are hurt; keeping close to God, your family, and godly people even when you're sad and in pain—that is hunkering down. This world hurts, that's for sure. Storms come and go, good days are amazing and bad days are terrible, but hunker down. Be tough. Don't give up.

Hold 'Em High

Your shoulders, cute little things they are, hold your arms on to your body (as we've already established). And sometimes, glorifying God with your shoulders means holding those arms in the air.

Use your shoulder to raise your hand and ask a question. Is there a question in your mind that you want the answer to? Whether at home, at school, at church, or on a sports team? Anywhere? Then ask.

Use your shoulders to raise your hands and dance around. Because, honestly, there isn't much that feels as totally awesome as a dance party. In fact, just last week some college girlfriends and I got together. After a dinner of cheeseburgers, fries, and puppy chow, we danced. Literally, in the living room, we just danced like we were crazy folks. 'Cause it's fun. And easy. And relaxing. And hilarious. The friendships in that room, the moments of total freedom to be silly, throwing our hands up and spinning around the room—it all glorified God. (Um, and please tell me you love puppy chow. The recipe is in the appendix, but let me warn you. It is *completely addicting*. And delicious.)

You can also use your shoulders to hold up someone else. Just thinking about this, my brain is immediately drawn to a story in the Old Testament about Moses.

In Exodus 17:11–13, as long as Moses held up the staff in his hand, the Israelites had the advantage. But whenever he dropped his hand, the Amalekites gained the advantage.

Moses's arms soon became so tired he could no longer hold them up. So Aaron and Hur found a stone for him to sit on. Then they stood on each side of Moses, holding up his hands. So his hands held steady until sunset. As a result, Joshua overwhelmed the army of Amalek in battle.

I have a friend, Kate, who just got out of a really painful relationship with a dude. You know the kind—where the girl cries herself to sleep for a couple of days in a row, needs friends around her all the time, and can hardly lift her head from the sofa cushion. She's in love with this guy, even though he wasn't a good boyfriend *at all*. I can understand that it's easy to fall in love with someone. But she's done with this relationship and wants to move on.

What is my role as Kate's friend? It's funny, because I think my role is a lot like Aaron's. Kate wants to be strong and stay away from the boy who hasn't loved her well. But it's hard to be that strong alone. So she depends on God and rallies her friends around her to literally be her strength. When her shoulders can no longer win the battle for her alone, some other girls and I step in and hold them up for her. And she will win. She will recover from the hurt of the breakup, and maybe we have influenced her to eat a bit too much ice cream, but we'll stand by her until the battle is done. We'll be strong when she can't be. Hold her up when her strength is gone.

Breakups are horrible. Not getting into the college or club or sorority or chorus that you wanted is horrible. And being strong alone is really hard. There are days when I'm not strong—about any number of topics (being single, finances, friendships, etc.)—and on those days, when I still want to fight the good fight with Christ, I hold up my arms as long as I can. But I also have to let my friends help—by sitting by me, crying with me, and holding me up, especially in prayer.

"Put Your Head on My Shoulder"

Seriously. Do songs from the fifties ever get old? I contend that they do not. Paul Anka may not be your particular guru, but he got this line right.

I have a rather embarrassing story related to putting heads on shoulders, and though my pride says to keep it to myself, the side of me that loves funny stories cannot resist sharing it.

The summer between my junior and senior years in high school, I met a guy named Steve. I met him on a local missions trip—one where you build things and clean up and all around look gross. Except for Steve. He was a football player at his high school, and let me tell you, that dude was strong. And big. And I had a crush on him about forty-five seconds after seeing him lift an armchair over his head and throw it into a dumpster. I decided right there that I didn't care where he was going to college (UCLA) or where he was from (Ohio), I would follow him to the ends of the earth (I didn't).

But we did take a break from the missions trip work to drive to Atlanta and go to Six Flags theme park. I do not prefer roller coasters, but that dislike paled in comparison to how much I wanted to be around Steve. (I really hope Steve never reads this book.)

We survived a few different rides and walked around doing that awkward flirting ritual—where we walked beside each other for a minute and then played it cool and went to stand by someone else. Oh, I was the epitome of a good flirter that day (yeah, right). At one point, our whole group sat down, and Steve and I ended up sitting beside each other. And by "ended up," I mean, "I finagled my way around our friends so that it looked like a coincidence that Steve and I were sitting together, but in reality I had made it work out." If you're a girl, then I *know* you can relate. We are masterful at creating these kinds of events.

So there we were, sitting beside each other on the rock wall. This memory is so awkward and clear that I think we could go to Six Flags in Atlanta today, more than ten years later, and I could still show you the exact spot where this event happened.

It was the middle of July, so it was *hot*. Did I mention that? 'Cause this makes the story so much better. So, it was really hot, and we were sitting right beside each other. Sticky. Sweaty. All the things that make an awkward boy-girl interaction so much more hilarious. And suddenly I realized that Steve's hat was touching my shoulder. But it wasn't like his head was *on* my shoulder—it was like he had bent his neck to a ninety-degree angle and pushed the top of his hat into the top of my arm.

Have you ever seen two people sitting directly beside each other, the football player dude with his head completely sideways into the girl's shoulder? Listen, I could have died, I was so embarrassed. It was the strangest situation, and if I could have run away, I totally would have. I couldn't. I'm being serious when I say that every time I think about heads on shoulders, I go back to this moment in my life and am so glad it happened. 'Cause it's funny. And awkward. Which is sometimes the best kind of funny.

But when talking about glorifying God with our bodies, letting someone rest their head on your shoulder is something totally different. It's being a good friend; it's being a place of healing. It's being a place of rest for someone who is hurt or sad or lonely.

I cannot even begin to count all the times I have needed my friends' shoulders throughout the years. Sometimes I literally just needed a place to rest my head because the world or my school or another friend or a boy had totally broken my heart and worn me out emotionally. Do you know that feeling? The moments when you don't need anyone to "say" anything; you just need a friend.

I remember one specific experience with a coworker. This girl and I had been friends for a long time, and one day she got mad at me. *Really* mad. The kind of mad when your face turns red and you start yelling and saying things that you later regret. She said a lot of things that broke my heart. The conversation ended, and I asked my boss if it was okay for me to go ahead and clock out. Seeing the mascara on my cheeks and the tears still forming in my eyes, he let me leave. I drove straight to Molly's house. She and I had been best friends for a while—and still are to this day. We sat on her couch and watched TV, and I cried. Sometimes she would hug me, but mostly she just let me sit there. Because I'm not a real touchy-feely person, I didn't lay my head on her shoulder.

But emotionally, that's what she did for me—she was a strong place where I could be hurt and try to heal. I don't remember what we watched; in my mind's eye the television is blurry from my tears. But what I remember clearly is how safe I felt and how loved I was in that moment. Did it heal my heart completely? Or heal the friendship with my coworker? No. But it calmed the storm in my heart for that little bit of time. And then, for the weeks that followed, Molly stood beside me, like Aaron and Hur did for Moses, as I hunkered down and let God finish the painful experience that had begun.

Not only is it good to offer your shoulder to your Christian girlfriends, it's also one of the best ways to reflect Jesus to your other friends. Because if you are anything like me, you have friends who aren't Christians. Even if you're nothing like me, you should have some friends who aren't Christians.

There are so many words you can say to them about Jesus, about how He loved them enough to die so that they could be forgiven for their sins. But those are just words. When you love your friends, even in their hurt, and hold them when they cry, and comfort them when they are brokenhearted, they see Jesus in you. Just as the old saying goes, actions speak far louder than words. As your unsaved friends experience the love of God through you, the opportunities to talk about God will come. Your life and your love will remind them of something far greater than yourself.

There are also times when the best way to glorify God with your shoulders is knowing when *not* to offer them. I think it needs to be said here that your shoulder isn't the best place for your guy friends. Sure, you may see them hurt and want to help. In fact, I just got an email that my friend Sam's dad passed away. I texted Sam to say I was praying for him, and I will. Do I rush to his house and hug him for hours? No. That role belongs to other guys in his life—the dudes in his small group and on his sports team, and the pastors in his life. When someone is hurt, boy or girl, a lot of emotions are involved, and though you may not love this truth, the reality is that being the strong place physically for your guy friends isn't the wisest thing to do. You can pray for them, email them, or write on their Facebook wall, but you can't be the shoulder they cry on. That isn't what's best for him. Or you.

Who knew shoulders were so important? I mean, sure, I appreciate that my arms most likely are not going to fall off at any point today, but spiritually and emotionally, the shoulders are actually very important instruments of righteousness. So if you are slouching, you better cut that out. Stand tall. Be proud. You've got some cute shoulders there, girl!

chew on this

Ponder:

Think of ways, in each of these categories, that you can glorify God with your shoulders:

1. Stand tall

2. Hunker down

3. Hold 'em high

4. Rest your head on my shoulder

Read:

Deuteronomy 33:12 (Does that seem safe to you? Why or why not?)

Isaiah 9:6 (What does this mean about Jesus?)

Look up:

shoulder, rest, strength

Do it:

Fix that posture, sister.

chapter 7

Heart

Things are about to get really personal up in here. Because no part of me is more central to who I am, and what I struggle with, than my heart. Don't you agree? No other place feels like the deeper core of me. So when I tell you stories from my heart that involve my heart, I sort of feel like I'm lying on a table, cut open, and you are the gallery standing around and looking at my guts.

Now, I know that isn't true, and you are not looking at my guts, but it feels that vulnerable. My heart is more than just a block of flesh pumping blood throughout my body, though I'm very grateful it does that too. In fact, let's all pause a minute and take our pulses as an act of appreciation for our hearts. What's your pulse, exactly? It's the number of times your heart beats in one minute.

So here's how to take your pulse:

1. Place the tips of your index, second, and third fingers on the palm side of your other wrist, below the base of the thumb. Or place the tips of your index and second fingers on your neck on either side of your windpipe.

2. Press lightly with your fingers until you feel the blood pulsing beneath them. You might need to move your fingers around slightly (up or down) until you feel the pulsing.

3. Use a watch with a second hand, or look at a clock with a second hand.

4. Count the beats you feel for ten seconds. Multiply this number by six to get your heart rate (pulse) per minute.

For me, today, in those ten seconds, my heart beat thirteen times. So my heart rate is seventy-eight. Right on track, which I expected. I'm just sitting here on my bed, my hair is still wet from my shower, and I'm listening to the calm crooning of Evan Wickham as I type. The normal rate for anyone over the age of eighteen is sixty to one hundred. So I'm sitting right in the normal zone, which is nice for a change, because it's not often I'm considered "normal." I'm just sayin'.

What about you? What is your heart rate?

Does it amaze you a little bit what you're counting there? Literally how many times your heart pumps blood to the rest of your body. That just really amazes me. Your little, hardworking heart is about the same size as your fist, and it weighs about the same as two baseballs. Cool, huh? So today we take a minute to be grateful that our hearts are pumping blood throughout our bodies and keep us going every day.

The human heart has four chambers. Now I've never been a star when it came to science, but I'm going to explain the heart as best I can. There are two atriums where the blood enters your heart. The right atrium brings in blood from all over the body, and the left atrium brings in blood from the lungs. (How are we doing so far? Okay?) The atriums are the top two chambers. Under the atriums are the ventricles. The right ventricle pumps blood out of the heart to the lungs, and the left ventricle pumps blood out of the heart to the whole body. So there are two chambers that allow blood into the heart, and two chambers that push blood out of the heart. Honestly, it is amazing that your body goes through that pumping process over one hundred thousand times a day! Wow.

But the heart I'm talking about here isn't just your physical way-to-pump-a-lot heart. I'm also talking about your inner heart, the place in you that you know so well. Oh, come on, girls, you know what I'm talking about—the secret place that houses your inner deepest wants, your secret crushes, and those most painful memories and hurts. *That* heart. That's the one we want to focus on here, because that heart is the core of who you are as a person—as *you*. Everyone's physical heart looks pretty much the same, but your core, your inner heart, looks as unique as a blade of grass or a snowflake. (But, as you know, I don't know much about snowflakes because I am a Southern belle. But I am going off the research I have read … written by people who live in the colder parts of the world, I am sure.)

I tend to think that our inner heart is built kind of like our physical heart. There are places for the things we allow into our hearts and places for the things we send out of our hearts. The challenge comes in how we handle what comes in and out of these chambers. We're going to use the four chambers of our physical heart to understand how God wants us to glorify Him with our whole emotional and spiritual heart.

The Right Atrium

Blood enters your heart from all over your body, like love enters your heart from all over your world.

When I think about blood entering your heart from your body, I think of all the different places that means—blood from the tips of your toes and behind your eyeballs and the lining of your stomach. So much variety. So it is with the world we live in—there are so many different things that want to get into your heart. Some of them are so very good: Love from your friends and family. Dreams of your future. Love and concern for people on earth who are less fortunate than you. Burdens for people you love. You watch the outside world and bring into your heart the things that are important to you.

Part of glorifying God with your heart is keeping it open to receive from the people around you. What does that look like exactly? Well, for each of us it will be a little different. But some practical examples include talking to your friends when you hurt, accepting compliments and receiving them in love, letting others serve you, and allowing yourself to cry on someone else's shoulder. Let people love you.

The good thing is that there are these little valves at the entrance to the right atrium so that the heart isn't overwhelmed with blood. They're like a protective door. For where you are in life, and where I am in life, this may be the most important part about glorifying God with your heart—protecting it.

Proverbs 4:23 puts it like this:

> Above all else, guard your heart, for everything you do flows from it.

Your heart is a wellspring of life, as some translations say— what flows out of it can bring life to all the people around you. (We're gonna chat about that in a minute.) But the main command here is to *guard your heart*. In real life, what does guarding your heart mean?

I used to get so frustrated at conferences and talks when speakers would tell me to "guard your heart" and then not tell me how to do it. Lame! But when I sat down and tried to write out how to do it, I couldn't explain how either. I mean, I can look at my friends' lives, and at my own life, and give you examples of what it looks like and what it feels like to guard your heart. But, unfortunately, that doesn't really do the topic justice. I want to be able to give you an A-B-C answer.

But as is the nature of the heart, there's always a bit of mystery involved and a bit of confusion. For weeks now, I've asked myself the question, how do I guard my heart? And I've found there are not adequate words to explain it. So today, as I sat frustrated, head in hands, at a coffee shop and stared at the blank pages, my friend Matt walked up. "Finished yet?" he asked.

"Not even," I replied, "It's this same chapter on the heart. I don't know how to tell them how to guard theirs."

Matt said, "Have you asked any other women how they do it?"

And I realized in that moment that I'm kind of an idiot. Because of course the better way to explain how to guard your heart is to give you a wide variety of thoughts from godly women on how they do it. So I sent an email, begging for help, to some single friends, married friends, moms, teens, college girls—all of them. Of all the responses, two major things popped out:

1. *Everyone* thinks guarding your heart is hard, and it's tough to define. (Phew! I'm not the only one!)

2. Guarding your heart looks different for each person, but the common response is that God has to direct you.

Here are a few of the answers I got. I learned a lot from them, and I think you will too.

- My friend Jennifer, who has a teenage daughter, said that we should keep wise women around us (I agree!) and not talk about boys all the time, 'cause it will get our hearts all aflutter. (Which I admit is a weakness of mine, so this was good to hear!)

- My wise twenty-five-year-old friend Lucy said guarding your heart means being patient and waiting for the right man. (Yep, I agree with that too!)

- My married writer friend Sarah Markley says that it's important to be careful not just with boys but with *things*—pursuits, dreams, etc. (Okay, I admit it, Sarah is super smart.)

- Caren, who works with a campus ministry at the University of Georgia, said that the key is remembering that you can be led by your emotions, but emotions can also deceive you. (So guarding your heart is identifying how you're handling your emotions? Got it.)

- I think Lee put it really well when she reminded me that God has to be *first*. Guarding your heart is loving Him more than anyone else.

I sat in the living room of a married couple today and asked them both what they'd say to young women about guarding their hearts. The husband said, "Girls should guard their hearts because it attaches value to who they are." I like that thought. Attach value to your heart by keeping it rare, special, and protected. That includes your personal stories.

I learned this firsthand very recently. As in last week. I realized that if I want to guard my heart, my guy friends don't get to hear every story of heartbreak or sadness or excitement in my life. My friend Stephen and I were hanging out so much that I was telling him every experience that came to mind. And with each story I related, we got to be closer friends. Which is fine—*to a point*. Then you either have to fish or cut bait—either date or not. And since he's not asking me out, I have to back off. He doesn't get every story. The stories from my heart? They are coming from a wellspring of *life*. Guarding my heart this week has meant closing my mouth and not letting every story spill out.

annie f. **downs**

Here's the truth: the best way to guard your heart is to surround yourself with other women who are able to do it. Women who live their lives in front of you and honor God with their hearts. You know who they are. Now you know who mine are too. These women—the ones who took time out of their busy days to answer my question? They are the voices of wisdom that teach me how to guard my heart.

As I was praying about guarding my heart, I was reminded of my favorite cartoon movie, Disney's *Beauty and the Beast.* It's a fantastic story that will make you give every dude you meet a second glance. Sing with me, 'cause you know you can: "There's something sweet and almost kind, but he was mean and he was coarse and unrefined." Ahhhh … I love that song.

Anyway, I was reminded of that part in the movie—centered around the sparkling rose kept protectively in a glass case. When Belle reached to touch the flower, the Beast slammed the glass down and growled angrily at her. That rose was his most prized possession, and he protected it with all his might. And his fur. That dude had a lot of fur.

So I've prayed, for years, that God would keep my heart as close to Him as the Beast kept that rose—protecting it with the same care, concern, and passion. Guarding your heart means recognizing that not everyone deserves to touch it or hold it or have it. Your heart is precious, your dreams should only be shared with a few close friends, and you should love well but carefully. You need to allow love into your heart but always remember to guard and protect it.

The Left Atrium

Blood enters your heart from your lungs, like love enters your heart from God.

God loves to love you. He's really good at it too. I like to think that every time I take a breath, and every time my lungs pump blood into my heart, God has another loving thing to say about me. He's that good at it. The breath of God, breathing life into your life, is full of love for you—no matter what you have done or where you have been, no matter what has been done to you or all the ways you feel like a screwup. Just like you don't decide how your blood flows, your behavior doesn't decide the flow of God's love into your heart. And for someone like me, that is pretty good at messing up and feeling guilty, it's really, really good to know that I can't make God love me any more or any less.

Just like the right atrium, the left atrium has a valve, or doorway, that protects the heart from receiving too much blood from the lungs. Yet here's the thing with God. The love and good things He wants to pour into your heart? The desires? The gifts? The plans? Girl, they will *never* be too much! Again, the spiritual valve is there for your protection. Here's the thing with God: He wants to pour so many good things into your life—His love, His desires, His gifts, His plans. How could they ever be too much? And yet He put a valve in your heart for your protection. Because, I'll be honest, if God poured out all those good things—the full measure of His love, His gifts, and His plans—on you at one time, I think you'd explode. So while the valve on the right protects you from too much input from the world and from the wrong kind of love, the valve on the left protects you from too much of God's awesome love at once. Nice thought, huh?

When I felt God calling me to move to Nashville, I wanted all the details. I wanted to know who my friends would be and who would hang out with me, where I would go to church, and where I would work and live. I wanted every tiny detail because I didn't want to take a step without knowing that the ending was a good one.

Have you ever had guy friends who loved to watch ESPN Classics? You know, the channel that shows football games from 1981? Yeah, I think that is totally ridiculous. I mean, seriously. The game is *way* over, and in most cases the dudes playing are dads lounging on their couches right now. I love watching football, but the games where I already know the result are totally boring to me. Why? Because my heart is totally uninvolved. I know the ending, so I have zero expectations or hopes.

God puts a valve on our hearts, the part that receives from Him, because to get everything from Him at one time would take away so much of the excitement and anticipation that's involved in the process of lovingly leading us.

So even though I don't know the ending to my story in Nashville, or even the ending to this day in Nashville, my heart is involved because of the mystery. Because I don't know what good things He has planned for today, I'm looking for Him around every corner. And all the good things I do have—awesome friends, a great small group, a cute house to live in—they have all entered the part of my heart that reminds me how much God loves me.

Allow God into your heart. Let Him into those little places inside that are still hurt and alone. Talk to Him about the secrets of your heart, knowing that He is fully trustworthy and that you don't need to guard your heart from Him, ever. Let Him love you, lead you, and make you into the person He has planned—because that adventure will be, I promise, the greatest of your life.

The Right Ventricle

Blood pumps out of your heart into your lungs like love pumps out of your heart into God's heart.

You seriously don't want me to even get started on this. I'm sitting in a public coffee shop, and I will all out ugly cry right here in front of all these people if we get to talking too much about loving God. But let me tell you what *sending* love to God looks like for me: THIS RIGHT HERE. Writing. Talking about Him. Expressing my love to Him in the life I live, the people I love, and the causes I serve. I want to live my life in a way that always and forever pumps as much love out of my heart and into God's as I can. Do I make mistakes? Constantly and absolutely. Am I a sinner? You better believe it, sister. But every day, for the rest of the time the Lord gives me on earth, I want my entire life to love Him.

Jason Morant wrote a song to express how he felt about God, and the chorus says, "My life's a love song to You."[2] I believe that deep in my heart. But why?

---

2. Jason Morant's album *Abandon* is totally worth the purchase. I'm just sayin'.

Because He is my everything. He loved me when I was totally and fully unlovable. In my deepest pit of sin, in the farthest corner of my rebellion, in the angriest moment of my hate, He chose to love *me*. And I've been known to be a total punk. Unfortunately, I will probably continue to be a punk at times. Yet He loves me to pieces—all my pieces. I cannot earn it, I don't deserve it, and yet I am drowning in it. So I do the little bits that I can to love Him back—and you can do the same. What does that look like? Well, it's perfectly unique (you're welcome) for each of us. Do you love to sing? Sing a love song to God. Do you love to write? Write a book about your love for God. Do you love to dance? Draw? Play sports? Care for orphans or elderly people? However you love to love, do it for the glory of God. THAT is loving Him back.

The Left Ventricle

Blood pumps out of your heart to the body like love pumps out of your heart to the world.

When I asked my friend Beth how she glorifies God with her heart, she said, "I think God is most glorified with my heart when I am living out of it. When my life portrays the things He has put within my heart, and they shine for all the world to see, then He must be glorified."

I have some smart friends, right? It's pretty unfair to the rest of the world that all of these wonderful women surround me. Loving the world means living out of the things God has placed in your heart and striving to become who He has always planned for you to be.

Last night I went to hear a musician perform. My friend Bethany played violin/fiddle for this artist, who was trying to land a new manager and get signed. Though Bethany and I have been friends for a few months now, this was the first time I saw her perform. I went to the show with my friends Jason and Keith. The three of us stood against the back wall, listening and watching as Bethany rocked that violin and sang some seriously high background vocals. She wore a supercute purple shirt, skinny jeans, and leg warmers. I didn't know that leg warmers were coming back in, but I think I'm actually okay with it. I know Annie 1987 is okay with it; I used to love those things.

A lightbulb moment occurred while I stood there listening to this girl sing about her brother loving macaroni and cheese (welcome to the undiscovered country talent of Nashville). The only four people I knew in that room were living out of their hearts and making real job choices out of their heart's desire.

Bethany plays violin full-time. At the show last night, she was fully engaged in the moment, feeling every note under her calloused fingers, her wrist surely becoming sore from moving the bow back and forth over the strings, and dancing from one end of the stage to the other. Bethany is doing the job that makes her heart beat, the profession she loves and through which she glorifies God.

Jason stood next to me. He's the tour manager for another local musician. He wrangles all his amazing organizational skills together to book hotels, count merchandise, and drive a van across the country just so someone else can be successful.

His heart is for his job and for serving other people in a way that honors them. He once said to me, "I do my job so that other people can do theirs." That is a giver, my friends.

Keith is a longtime employee of Compassion International, a nonprofit organization that helps children all over the world to receive the education and care they need to become productive adults in society. Keith has a heart for the poor of the world, and picked a job where that is the focus.

And then there's me. Former elementary-school teacher and current author, who quit her stable, secure, and money-guaranteed job to do what her heart loves—writing for girls like you. Speaking to girls like you. Living my life so that girls like you will see Jesus in the everyday.

It was funny to stand there, our little line of friends with abnormal jobs, and think about what it looks like to live out of your heart. If you've protected your heart and allowed God to fill it with His plans and love, then you can trust your desires. So as you age and get to pick who you want to be and what you want to do, pray, seek God, and trust the desires He has put in your heart. Loving the world means being who God has planned for you to be, so you can touch and impact all those around you.

Whew! The heart. Y'all I am about to jump out of my chair, I'm so excited about what you have to gain from this chapter. For that matter, what I have to gain from this chapter! My heart rate is now ninety, and I'm not one bit surprised.

chew on this

Ponder:

> Who in your life is a good example of how to guard your heart?

> How can you guard your heart?

> How can you show your love for God?

> How can you show love to the world around you?

> Think about each chamber of the heart and its function—is it easier to let things flow into your heart or out of your heart?

> Which chamber is the most difficult?

> What makes it easy or difficult for you?

Read: Psalm 4:7; Song of Songs 2:7; Ezekiel 11:19; Luke 2:19

Look up: *heart, love*

Do it:

> Ask one woman in your life what it looks like to guard your heart.

chapter 8

Hands

Your hands are serious business. Just ask the Centers for Disease Control and Prevention. Pages and pages of their website are dedicated to hand hygiene. They make it rather clear that it is extremely important to keep your hands clean. And when I say "extremely important," I think the CDC would say "life or death."

To be precise, when I typed the keyword "hands" into the cdc.gov search box, it spit back ten thousand different documents. Looking through some of these, I noticed they even have downloadable PowerPoint slide shows that show exactly how and when to wash your hands. My perspective is that if you're able to use PowerPoint, you should be able to wash your hands correctly. (But that's a personal opinion.)

Nonetheless, I feel it's important to share with you that basic information. Though it isn't exactly our topic for today, the thought that a friend doesn't know *when* or *how* to wash their hands is disturbing. I would be doing you an injustice if I didn't include the following hand-washing procedures:

- Wet your hands with clean running water and apply soap. Use warm water, if available.

- Rub hands together to make a lather and scrub all surfaces.

- Continue rubbing hands for twenty seconds. Need a timer? Imagine singing "Happy Birthday" twice through to a friend!

- Rinse hands well under running water.

- Dry your hands using a paper towel or air dryer. If possible, use your paper towel to turn off the faucet.

So, when should you wash your hands? According to the CDC,

- Before, during, and after preparing food

- Before eating food

- Before and after caring for someone who is sick

- Before and after treating a cut or wound

- After going to the bathroom

- After changing diapers or cleaning up a child who has gone to the bathroom

- After blowing your nose, coughing, or sneezing

- After handling an animal or animal waste

- After touching garbage[3]

At the top of this particular CDC webpage, it says "Clean Hands Save Lives!" Interesting, isn't it? All this, someone's full-time job at the CDC, just to make sure we take care of our hands. Believe it or not, I even came across a website for the Clean Hands Campaign. (Seriously? An entire campaign just to get us to wash our hands? Wow.)

There must be something to this. Why are our hands so susceptible to disease? Why do our hands carry enough power to *save lives*?

Here's the answer: our hands are in *everything*. Our hands are powerful. There really isn't any activity we do on a regular basis that doesn't somehow involve our hands. Think about it—writing, eating, typing, driving, cleaning, dancing, playing, and even (for many people) talking. All these activities are made complete with our hands. Try to think of something that *doesn't* involve your hands. I don't think I can.

The kindest people on earth use their hands to bless and help people. Mothers holding their babies, nurses changing the bandages on their patients, volunteers handing out food at a homeless shelter. On the other hand (pun totally intended), the evilest of people also use their hands to accomplish what they want to do—murder, rape, torture, steal, and other horrible things.

---

3. If you want to check it out yourself, all this handwashing info comes from a CDC report: "Handwashing: Clean Hands Saves Lives," February 8, 2012, www.cdc.gov/handwashing/

Our hands have the power to achieve such good and yet such evil. That interests me. I think it's all part of the free will God has given us, but the fact that most of our body parts have the ability to create and destroy is amazing.

I'm not the biggest fan of my hands. Let me give you a few reasons why. For starters, my fingers are chubby like little sausages. For seconds, I have dealt with the bad habit of biting my fingernails for the majority of my life, so at the ends of my sausage fingers are these little nubby nails. My palms have the tendency to get really sweaty without any warning. And I pop my knuckles. So all around, my hands are not my prize possessions. (Though I really am trying to quit biting my nails, because it just looks so gross most of the time.)

Remember, it's about being okay with our bodies, not necessarily being in love with them. So I figure if I can quit biting my nails, maybe I'll start to have a little more appreciation for my hands.

Our Clean Hands

Our goal since the beginning of this book has been to figure out what it looks like to make our body parts instruments of righteousness that glorify God. So, what do our hands need to do, and need to avoid, to be those instruments?

Just like the CDC, the Bible considers hands, and the use of them, very important. In fact, there are over five hundred verses in the Bible that refer to the use of hands. (Thank you, Biblegateway.com, for being so very good at what you do. Well done.) We look to the Bible not to learn how to wash our hands but to learn what clean hands are. Really clean hands. This has nothing to do with germs or baby poop; it has to do with the state of your heart. Your hands behave how your heart tells them to behave—they are responders, not initiators.

Look at Psalm 24:3–4:

> Who may ascend the mountain of the LORD? Who may stand in his holy place? The one who has *clean hands* and a pure heart, who does not trust in an idol or swear by a false god" (emphasis mine).

God requires that our hands be clean and our hearts be pure before we go before Him. But how do you keep your hands clean the way God requires? Because the Jewish leaders of that time took this verse literally, people had to wash their hands in the temple, and there were "unclean" things people couldn't touch. Though these leaders were legalistic to the tenth degree, I'm not sure I'm so against the idea of washing our hands at church. It would be an outward and visible sign of an inward spiritual truth: we are unclean. We don't deserve to come into the presence of the Lord. And no matter how hard we try, we cannot figure out a way to stay clean, spiritually or physically. We get dirty. We make bad choices. And we need to clean our hands. But we can't. I'm sorry to tell you, but you don't have the power to clean your hands. No matter how many times you sing "Happy Birthday" and scrub, your hands can never be clean enough for you to go before God.

Maybe that's one of the reasons Jesus was crucified and

the nails pierced His *hands*. The blood that ran down from His hands, from that very area that has to be clean, is what keeps us clean. When we accept Jesus, He trades His pure hands for our dirty ones. He is the only way we can be clean. This is hard for me. I think, "I can scrub hard enough," but I can't. I'm grateful that it is by His blood I am clean. No work for me. No glory for me.

So now we choose to honor Him with our hands. Knowing what He has done for us, how should we respond? I've come up with a few different ways we can glorify God with our hands.

Worship

First of all, let me say that you are allowed to worship however you choose. But God's Word says repeatedly to lift up our hands to Him in worship. Let's look at some of those verses:

> *Lift up your hands* in the sanctuary and praise the LORD."
>
> Psalm 134:2, emphasis mine

> I will praise you as long as I live, and in your name I will *lift up my hands*.
>
> Psalm 63:4, emphasis mine

> Hear my cry for mercy as I call to you for help, *as I lift up my hands* toward your Most Holy Place.
>
> Psalm 28:2, emphasis mine

My observation is that all of these verses are from the book of Psalms, and were likely written by King David. David was a worshiper. He liked to worship in unique ways (such as dancing practically naked in the streets). Though I don't necessarily agree with that particular method (but do your thang, girl), I do like his thought patterns. David just did whatever brought him closer to the Lord.

We communicate so much nonverbally. When we lift up our hands to God, we're not only worshiping Him, we're reaching out to Him and expressing our need for Him. Think about these things—when a baby wants a parent to pick her up, what does the baby do? *Lifts up her hands.* When someone is in the bottom of a pit and is screaming for help, what does he do? *Lifts up his hands.* Both are extending their hands to someone they hope can offer help.

The movie *Shawshank Redemption* comes to my mind. Remember the scene where Andy is finally free? It's pouring rain, and he is standing in mud, crying. And where are his hands? Stretched straight out. A symbol of his freedom. Of his lack of chains.

So lift up your hands, girl! There are so many different emotions you can express by lifting up your hands. No matter what your heart is feeling, it's good to lift up your hands to God. To praise Him, to worship Him, to cry out to Him, to give up our problems to Him.

Loving Touch

As I mentioned earlier, I'm not a touchy-feely kind of girl in general. But I will say that there is something powerful in touch. When Jesus touched people, what happened? They were healed. There is power in a loving touch.

Several years ago I led a missions trip that was really high stress. We had sick team members and mean team members, and I was only twenty years old, in charge of twenty other people. And none of them were my friends. I mean, I knew them from college, but none of my closest girlfriends had come on the trip. So I was basically alone. Except for one friend—Bert. Bert already lived in the city we were in, so our team was staying in his home.

One morning, while the team was still asleep, I got up with my Bible and journal and headed to the kitchen. Sitting at the table, I wrote and wept, out of exhaustion and sadness and loneliness. I heard the metal chair beside me move and I looked up to see Bert sitting down with me. Without saying a word, Bert reached his hand across the table and held mine. We weren't dating, it wasn't like that at all; it was just one friend supporting another friend in a time of desperate need. I have never forgotten that act of kindness, the lack of unnecessary words, and the total healing that came from just a small gesture of touch.

Here's another example of healing from touch:

> On a Sabbath Jesus was teaching in one of the synagogues, and a woman was there who had been crippled by a spirit for eighteen years. She was bent over and could not straighten up at all. When Jesus saw her, he called her forward and said to her, "Woman, you are set free from your infirmity." *Then he put his hands on her*, and immediately she straightened up and praised God."

> Luke 13:10–13, emphasis mine

One of my favorite praise songs keeps running through my mind. I can't get it out. It's called "He Touched Me," and it was written by Bill Gaither. The chorus says,

He touched me,
Oh, He touched me,
And oh the joy that floods my soul.
Something happened and now I know,
He touched me and made me whole.

Jesus's touch does more than heal. It makes us whole! Hallelujah! Science has proven over and over again the positive effects on infants who are repeatedly touched. In fact, one researcher's report I read found that growth and mental development in babies is improved by touch. The earlier the touch, the better the effects. Touch also helps improve sleep conditions for the little ones. The same goes for us. When someone takes time to touch you, hug you, pat your back, even just rest his or her hand on yours, it creates something positive in you. It blesses you. It grows in you.

Before we go on, though, I probably need to mention this. All touch isn't appropriate touch. And I bet all of us, myself included, can think of times when we were touched in an unloving way, in a fighting way, a sexually abusive way, or a hateful way. In fact, what does your mind automatically do when you read the words "when someone takes time to touch you"? For many of us, it brings up unpleasant thoughts. But we're talking about clean hands here. If you've been treated unfairly by someone else's hands, you need to deal with that. Or even if you've touched someone in an unloving way in the past (I have—ask my sister Tatum! She's been punched more times than she can remember), that doesn't dictate the behavior of your hands in the future. In fact, your hands, as well as your heart, have been forgiven and redeemed through Jesus.

Loving touch is all good. Babies grow because of loving touch. Friendships grow because of loving touch. Touch can calm us down or excite us. I love holding babies and hugging high schoolers. As a teacher, I used the power of touch often. When a student fell down, I wanted to hug him. When a little girl cried because someone hurt her feelings, I wanted to hug her. That kind of touch is healing. I also used touch to calm someone down or to redirect their behavior. One tap on the shoulder of a hyper child gave the signal that they had reached their limit (or my limit). It's crazy to think that I am worshiping God in those moments, but it's true.

Look at Mark 10:16:

And he [Jesus] took the children in his arms, placed his hands on them and blessed them.

One of my students from a few years ago, Paul, came up to my desk *a lot*. When he got there, he often couldn't remember why he came. He would say, "Holda holda holda," meaning, "Hold on while I attempt to recall that which I was going to say to you." Then he'd just stand there smiling and rolling his eyes at his own forgetfulness. Usually I grabbed his hand when he walked up and held it while his brain worked to remember. The one time I didn't, he stared at me and didn't say a thing.

I said, "Yes, Paul? Have you forgotten what you were going to say?" Then I realized that I wasn't holding his hand. I grabbed it, and usual behavior returned, including his big grin and his made-up word, "Holda." I suddenly realized that Paul didn't always come to my desk because he had something to say. He came to my desk because he liked the love I gave him when I held his hand.

Touching can get sticky, though, because not everyone loves to be touched. Some people don't respond as well to it. I am one of those people, to be honest. So our job, as instruments of righteousness, is to trust the Lord to lead us, even in this. Touch can be powerful. Remember, Jesus healed with His hands, He set people free from sin and demons with His hands, and He raised people from the dead with His hands. Allow the Lord to guide your hands.

Serving People

I will never forget the tsunami that hit Southeast Asia in 2004. We were out of school for Christmas break. When we returned, the students in my class had many questions and a desire to do something to help. Through the Red Cross, we found that we could donate money to provide people shelter and food. So we started a change drive. Kids from all over our school would bring change and drop it in a jar. On Fridays we would bring the jar to our room and pour the money out onto the floor. One table of students collected quarters, another dimes, another nickels, and another pennies. Then they would roll the coins. Would you believe that in a single month we raised more than one thousand dollars? (And not one cent was pocketed by my students.) We were able to provide more than twenty family-sized tents for people in Asia. When the change drive began, I would not have believed that we would have that outcome, especially when twenty-five fifth graders were leading the charge. But with their sweet hands, they rolled money and collected money and wrote notes to send home to parents all over our school. They were servants. And God was honored by their hands.

There are many ways to serve people—going to a homeless shelter and volunteering to serve a meal, going to India and hugging orphans, going to Costa Rica and helping build a church, going anywhere in the world, getting in the middle of their mess and helping clean it up.

One of the characteristics of a godly wife, which we all hope to be, is that "she opens her arms to the poor and extends her hands to the needy" (Proverbs 31:20).

I work with a nonprofit organization called the Mocha Club.[4] The Mocha Club helps educate, feed, heal, and serve Africans for donations of just a few dollars a month, about the cost of just two mochas. I walked into the Nashville office yesterday and saw my friend Betsy, who is a volunteer at Mocha. Piles of T-shirts surrounded her—I would guess at least five hundred. Without a word, and with no complaints, Betsy was folding the shirts perfectly and stacking them by size. The

---

4. Make sure you check out the Mocha Club and join my team at http://www.
themochaclub.org/sponsor/anniedowns

shirts will be shipped soon, all over the world, and the money will go directly toward Mocha Club's projects in Africa. Betsy used her hands to give to the needy people in Africa by folding shirts in Nashville. She was serving the Lord, and yet she never left our zip code.

It's great to be local in your serving—using your hands to care for people in your own city. But honestly, isn't it easier to do things for people across the world than to serve the ones who live in your house, or in your neighborhood?

You have the opportunity to begin using your hands as instruments of righteousness today. Right now. Try one of these ideas:

- Unload the dishwasher

- Clean your room

- Change your own sheets for once

- Do your best on every homework assignment

- Play baseball with your little brother

- Clap when your little sister performs a ballet in the living room (even if it's too long and mildly horrible)

- Mow the lawn

- Give someone a ride to school

- Hug your mom or dad

- Write a note to someone important to you, thanking them for being in your life

- Cook dinner for your family

The list could go on forever. Using your hands to serve people is about taking some time out of your life to focus on someone else. Making someone else more important than yourself.

Remember this scripture:

Whatever your hand finds to do, do it with all your might.

Ecclesiastes 9:10

Another way to serve people with your hands is by laying your hands on them when you pray for them. God has made it clear in His Word that when we lay hands on someone, His power flows through us into them. Many times, healing comes. Every time, His presence comes.

I remember the first time I ever prayed and laid my hands on someone to be healed. I was a freshman in college and was with a missions team in Costa Rica. We were at a family's house to eat dinner, and one of the children, who was deaf in one ear, asked us to pray for her. All of the adults went over to lay hands on her, and the team leader looked and beckoned me to come as well. I was shocked. And totally freaked out. I didn't know how to pray for someone to be healed! I had never done that before—what if it didn't work? I went anyway, scared out of my mind. We all laid hands on her, and we all prayed. To this day, I don't know if she is healed. But I know the Lord was right there with us, and she felt His presence. Maybe that was all she needed, really.

I love the story of Jesus healing the young girl in Mark 5. A man came to Jesus and told him his daughter was sick. He said to Jesus, "Please come and *put your hands* on her so that she will be healed and live" (verse 23, emphasis mine)." So Jesus agreed to go.

On the way, a woman who has a bleeding problem reached out and touched His cloak. You probably know the story. By the time that whole situation worked itself out, a messenger came and informed the man his daughter had died. Jesus told the man to believe and went with him anyway. We'll pick up the story at verse 40:

> [Jesus] took the child's father and mother and the disciples who were with him, and went in where the child was. *He took her by the hand* and said to her, "Talitha koum!" (which means, "Little girl, I say to you, get up!"). Immediately the girl stood up and walked around (she was twelve years old). At this they were completely astonished.
>
> Mark 5:40–42, emphasis mine

What did Jesus do? He used His hand, grabbed her hand, and raised her from the dead. Tell me that's not serving someone else!

Looking back at all of these ways to serve, it seems that our hands can be a bit overwhelming. There's a lot of power contained below your elbows. But there is also a lot of potential for freedom and forgiveness as well. Don't forget that.

Live your life in a way that shows that your hands truly are instruments of righteousness. Ask yourself, in each situation, if your hands—and your heart—are creating good things or destroying. Glorify God with your hands. Worship Him.

Good job reading all this—give yourself a hand. Ha!

chew on this

Ponder:

Read Joshua 4:24.

Identify places in Scripture or in your life that show how powerful the Lord's hands are.

Can you think of a way to use your hands to glorify God that wasn't discussed in this chapter?

Is there a way you can worship God with your hands in your home? At school? At church? In your city? In the world?

Remember, you are made in God's image—that means your hands are meant to reflect Him to the world too.

Read: Psalm 88:9; Psalm 119:48; Isaiah 55:12; James 4:8

Look up: *hands, touch, feel*

Do it:

Serve someone else this week with your hands. Allow the Lord to lead you to someone who could use a loving touch, and hug them. Also, if you have memories of being touched in an unloving way that you need to deal with, talk to someone you trust and get on the path to healing that area of your life.

chapter 9

Stomach

Sometimes this book gets all up in my business. Does that make any sense? I mean, there have been times in this research-and-writing phase when I don't even want to open a Word document because the topic I know I have to write about is too personal. It's too Annie. And it's too hard.

Hence the reason I'm doing the stomach chapter at the eleventh hour, when I really should be getting close to being completely finished with this book. I don't know that I know how to deal with this issue very well yet. The other chapters? I haven't mastered those issues yet either, but I feel like, "Hey, I'm thirty-one, I know a thing or two about this stuff. I bet this will help these cute girls work out their salvation a bit."

But when it comes to the stomach, I just have to be real with y'all. I don't have it down yet. I try, good gracious do I try, but it isn't an area where I see tons of victory. Yet. I want to real bad, and it's something that's on my heart and mind on a daily basis, but as far as saying, "Yay! I have it all figured out! I have all the answers you need!" ... well, I can't really say that yet.

I've struggled with my weight since fourth grade. Actually, maybe fifth grade. I remember fifth-grade Annie watching a video of fourth-grade Annie doing a presentation. I was in the basement of my house and I was lying on a beanbag chair. Someone in the room said, "Wow, Annie. Look how much thinner you were last year." And that's the first moment I thought I was fat. And on and off for the past twenty years, I've thought that. But honestly, weight isn't the biggest deal. It's a number. A pants size. That's all. The bigger concern is how I got here and why I can't get away from it.

As is the case with most every other body part, your stomach doesn't act alone. Quite the contrary. Without grossing us all out, we know that the stomach and the digestive system work hand in hand, as along with the mouth, the esophagus, and whatever else is connected down there. But in a deeper sense, the stomach is connected to the brain, and to the heart.

Because at some point in my life, food stopped being just food and started being a friend. Or an enemy. Either way, food got a big head and decided it was more than just fuel for my body. Food made the decision to be my companion, my release, or my archnemesis. Maybe all three.

I remember the only time in my entire life that I stole anything. (I hope I don't go to jail for telling this story.) I was in the seventh grade, and I was working the sixth-grade dance at our middle school. And by "working," that pretty much means I talked to my friends and stood behind the snack table. Were a lowly sixth grader to approach, I might stop my conversation, grab the kid's dollar, and toss a bag of M&M's somewhat in their direction. I was *way* too cool. (Yeah, right.) When the night ended, I remember my friend Ryan saying, "You know you can take the candy home, right? They don't care."

I knew better. I knew they would care. After the sixth-grade dance ended, my seventh-grade friends arrived for our own dance. And during the seventh-grade dance, someone hurt my feelings. And in case you don't remember, getting your feelings hurt in seventh grade is *severe drama*. And I was completely shattered ... for a twelve-year-old. So the idea of candy sounded great. (Which is dumb. Because first of all, I wasn't even hungry. Second of all, I didn't have any money. Third of all, how was candy supposed to make my heart feel better?)

Nevertheless, I took it. Two Hershey's bars and a bag of M&M's. I stuffed them into my book bag and left. As soon as I got home, I headed to my room and devoured that chocolate in minutes. Literally. I shocked even myself. Did I feel better? Nope. In fact, I felt guilty as sin (I was) and big as a cow (I wasn't).

The Devil Made Me Do It

Looking at the Bible, we can see where this issue with food began. And unfortunately, this problem, from the start, is a deeper struggle for girls than for boys. Does that mean that no dude on earth struggles with this? Not at all. There is no sin, and I mean *no sin*, that is gender specific. Even that one you're thinking of right now? Yup, *everybody* struggles.

Let's start at the very beginning with Eve. In Genesis 3, Satan, the snake, convinced Eve that she needed more to eat. Have you ever considered that? Satan used food to say, "What you have isn't enough; you need more. You are lacking something and this food will fill your need." Was it true? No. Adam and Eve had everything they could possibly have needed. God created the garden of Eden to satisfy them. In fact, God Himself walked around with them. Seriously, y'all. How is *that* not enough? And yet the snake was still able to tell Eve that to feel whole, to feel good, she needed more to eat.

Think of all the other ways the story could have gone—maybe he could have convinced her to drink. Or try a new exercise routine. Or shop too much at the local … uh … leaf clothing store? (I don't know … that's probably stretching it.) He didn't even try to get Eve to worship him—he could have said, "Pray to me and I will make you wise." He was, and is, more cunning than that. He knew she wouldn't straight out change teams—she wasn't an idiot. Eve wasn't going to start worshiping a snake. His goal wasn't to gain her worship personally, just to make sure she didn't worship God. So she might not become a Satan worshiper, but she'd eat. Do you see what I mean? Of all the things God created, it was *food* that the sneaky snake used to bring false comfort to Eve.

And his tactics haven't changed. That's one thing you can know for sure about the Enemy. It may feel like he's trying something new on you, but the Bible says "there is nothing new under the sun" (Ecclesiastes 1:9). So there is no lie Satan has told you that he hasn't fed to someone else before. Maybe even Eve herself.

Your poor stomach. You know, I kind of feel sorry for my stomach. What did it ever do to me to deserve to be mistreated? A whole lotta nothing. But my stomach is my whipping boy—the one who takes the punishment for the sins of another, usually my brain. Sometimes my heart. When my heart makes a mistake and gets hurt? My stomach gets fed. When my mind can't slow down? My stomach gets fed.

It's easy to dishonor our stomachs, because there are a variety of ways to do it. For example, we may overfeed them. We may underfeed them. We may punish them or reward them. We may love them too much or hate them. I think that's what makes this idea of glorifying God with our stomachs so hard—there are too many ways to do it wrong.

Lucky for you, and *super* lucky for me, God is way bigger than all of that. He created our stomachs to work for us, not against us. You have a stomach because your body depends on food to survive. How can you go into all the nations and share about Jesus if you don't have the strength that comes from a healthy diet? So let's start by wiping the slate clean with your stomach. Reintroduce yourself and make friends with it. Play nice. And remember, just like with every other body part, your stomach is there to help you glorify God, not make things harder.

Yummy!

If we're just talking mechanics, then you know that your stomach is necessary, because that's where the food you take in is digested. Then, as you digest the food, your body receives energy to move and do and be. So that's why we keep eating. That's why breakfast is so important. Getting food into your system when your body starts to move is vital. Your body has to have fuel to run on, and that fuel may look like a waffle with peanut butter at seven in the morning. Mmm ... I do love waffles with peanut butter. (Check the appendix for a little tip on this breakfast treat.) You have to feed your stomach. And you have to feed your stomach in a way that glorifies God. But how?

This is where God's love and grace in His creation amaze me. Because God made your stomach (and mine) in such a way that when you need food, your stomach tells you. And when you are full, your stomach tells you. So here's the answer to how you can glorify God with your stomach: you eat when you're hungry and you stop eating when you're full.

Easy directions, right? Just not so easy to follow. I'm pretty good at waiting until my stomach signals that it's hungry by growling. If it has been a while since you let yourself feel hunger, then it may take a little time. But just wait and eat when your stomach starts to growl. Don't wait until you feel like you're going to throw up because you're so hungry, but don't just eat because it's dinnertime. God made your stomach to signal when your body needs more nourishment.

When I was sixteen I decided to start listening to my body for hunger signs instead of just eating to eat. I stood in the kitchen stressed and concerned because my stomach wouldn't growl. I had been overfeeding my body so much, and my stomach had been silent for so long, that it had nothing to say. So it took almost a whole day before I was hungry! How crazy is that! But now I've trained my body to listen to my stomach, and I've spent significant time praying and asking God to help me in this area. It's not easy, y'all. But making your stomach an instrument of righteousness after you've trained it to be an instrument of destruction for so long is a bit of a challenge.

So it has taken time, but I have a decent grasp on waiting until I'm hungry to eat. And when that signal comes, I know I need to eat. Denying your bodies food when they need food to survive is a whole can of worms that we're going to open in just a minute. But learning to stop eating when I'm full isn't quite as simple. Because I was raised to believe in the "Clean Plate Club"—maybe you were too—and sometimes my brain says that everything on my plate should end up in my mouth, even if I'm unable to move after I eat. That plus living in a hurry-up culture sure makes it hard to sit and enjoy and savor a good meal. Instead I'm tempted to rush through, eat everything, and then ache for forty-five minutes afterward.

Honoring God with your stomach means giving it what it needs but not filling it so full that you're immobile. Your body doesn't need a huge amount of food to survive. In fact, many nutritionists say that it's actually better to eat six small meals a day because your body needs less food in more frequent increments. So wait until you're hungry, eat slowly and enjoy it, then stop when you're full.

Not So Delicious

Honoring God with your body means not giving it more than it needs or less than it needs. Many girls I know—okay, almost all the girls I know—struggle with how to feed their stomachs. They err on one side or the other. Either they don't feed them or they feed them too much.

Anorexia is a hard struggle. If you don't know, there are actually two types. One type of anorexia is simply medical—your body experiences a loss of appetite. This can happen when you're on certain medications or when you're sick. When I had my tonsils out at twenty-eight (nightmare!), I went a couple of days without really eating anything. I didn't have an eating disorder; my body was just healing, and the energy that normally went into digesting my food actually went into healing my body. This condition is labeled "anorexia," though it isn't what we commonly consider anorexia.

Anorexia nervosa isn't a medical disorder; it is an emotional disorder. (Here we go again with the stomach being connected to the heart and the mind.) It's an obsessive desire to lose weight by refusing to eat. Anorexia has so many faces. It doesn't mean that you never eat. Some people eat one meal a day, and that's all they allow themselves, while other people limit what they eat to one food group—maybe just crackers all day or just celery.

I grew up with a girl who only ate apples and pretzel sticks for the majority of our sophomore year of high school. I knew another girl in college who literally ate one meal a day—lunch—and that was it. That's anorexia. And it's real, it's ugly, and it's unwise. If you struggle with this, it is literally killing you slowly, and you need help. But it's not something you can do alone. You need to tell someone you trust and find help. (If you look in the appendix, there are some organizations you can contact. But also remember that there are people in your city, in your church, and probably in your home who are your best resources.)

On the other end of the spectrum is bulimia. *Bulimia* is defined as "an eating disorder characterized by uncontrolled rapid digestion of large quantities of food over a short period of time, followed by self-induced vomiting, fasting, and other measures to prevent weight gain."[5] In normal language, that just means eating way too much and then getting it back out of your body as quickly as possible. That is accomplished either through throwing up or using laxatives or any other method that removes food fast. Just like anorexia, bulimia isn't something you can beat on your own. So please, tell someone you love if you're struggling with this issue. (And again, there are organizations listed in the appendix you can contact.)

I remember being in eighth grade and getting a phone call from my friend Brittany. "Annie," she said, "I think I've figured out a way for us to lose weight before the dance in May." I was all ears. "We'll just take these pills that make you have diarrhea." And so for about a week, I did. Let me tell you, there is no more horrible experience. Did I lose weight? Barely. I felt horrible, my hair lost its shine, and my stomach was upset the entire time.

---

5. This definition comes from the *American Heritage Scientific Dictionary* (Houghton Mifflin Company. Taken from dictionary.reference.com/browse/bulimia)

Why? Why do we girls do this to ourselves? There are at least one hundred answers, and each girl probably has a different one. There's a lot to be said for our need to control, and I get that. Sometimes it feels as if the only thing we can control is what we eat (or don't eat). If your home life is chaotic, or if your family is going through a hard time, you especially may want to feel something is under your control.

But when we boil down all the reasons, it goes back to the same basic idea: we have forgotten, I had forgotten, maybe you have forgotten the truth. The truth about how God feels about us and how He made each of us wonderfully. We look around and see what we're "supposed" to look like, and then we sacrifice all to make it so. Or we throw in the towel and accept whatever we look like as our punishment. Or we try both options, as I did my entire teen life, flip-flopping between extreme dieting, extreme overeating, and extreme sadness.

So not only have I tasted these diseases on my own tongue, I've had friends struggle with both of them, and it's torture to watch. They get defensive, secretive, and sad. And there you stand, wishing you could help but having a hard time balancing between speaking truth and preserving friendship. It's a sticky situation when someone you love is sick. But you know as well as I do that you have to tell. Now is the time. Tell your parents. Tell your youth pastor. Tell someone you love and trust who also loves and trusts your struggling friend. You have to. You really do. I know, I'm sorry, it sucks to hear, but it's true. Be a part of the healing process.

If you're struggling with anorexia or bulimia, how do you

stop? First, tell somebody you trust, and it probably needs to be an adult. Please. And then go back to the Word and remember how God feels about you and how He made you. Spend some serious time in Psalm 139. Trust that God is in control, release your desire to be the boss (trust me, I know it's hard), and let God take care of you.

Tasty!

Maybe you don't struggle with an eating disorder or overeating or undereating. Because, honestly, there are some girls who don't really see food as an issue. Luckily, you still have a great opportunity to honor God with your stomach! It's important that you also make healthy choices for yourself. I'm not going to tell you what to eat, because you may not like the same things I do. (For example, I think peppers of all kinds are horrible, so I would say avoid them. But you peppa lovas out there may revolt against me, and I don't really want any anti-Annie protests going on.)

1 Corinthians 6:19–20 puts it pretty simply:

Do you not know that your bodies are temples of the Holy Spirit, who is in you, whom you have received from God? You are not your own; you were bought at a price. Therefore honor God with your bodies.

Your body is a temple. I'm sure you've heard that before. But let's put it in "for real" terms. What if you walked into church on Sunday to find that all the garbage trucks in the whole city had decided to put all the trash they collected on Saturday into your sanctuary? Can you imagine the shock on the people's faces? It would be *horrible*. The smell. The sound of crunching bags as people stepped all over the trash. And wouldn't you be so angry? The fact that the garbage company would even consider leaving piles of trash in a sanctuary is ludicrous.

That example isn't far from the truth of the situation with you. God lives in you; you are a sanctuary. If you're eating Funyuns and drinking a twelve pack of Coke every day, then you are pretty much dumping trash in your sanctuary.

Now we've already been over how I feel about ice cream. I heart it. A lot. But if I were to eat it every day, then there is no question that I would be filling my sanctuary with bags and bags of sticky, sweet trash. On the other hand, if I tried to convince you that I love eating a rabbit's diet, I would be lying. The ticket is to do all things in moderation. My struggle is, and has always been, overeating. I put what I want to eat above the truth of what my body needs to survive. But check out this next scripture. Paul was talking about people who are enemies of the cross. I don't know about you, but that is something I've tried to pretty consistently avoid. Yikes.

> For, as I have often told you before and now say again even with tears, many live as enemies of the cross of Christ. Their destiny is destruction, *their god is their stomach*, and their glory is in their shame. Their mind is set on earthly things.
>
> Philippians 3:18–19 (NIV 1984), emphasis mine

"Their god is their stomach"? That is a frightening thought, because I know for a fact that there are days when this is absolutely true about me. It's a battle, each day, to eat right and in moderation, not only the choices, but also the quantities. Cheese is okay to eat, but when you eat an entire block of Velveeta with crackers? Probably not so profitable.

God takes food pretty seriously. There are over three hundred different verses using the word *food* in the NIV translation of the Bible. That's a lot of delicious talking going on. And if God is so serious about this topic, I think we should be too. Glorifying God with your stomach means loving Him more than your next meal. Desiring to know Him more than you desire a cheeseburger. And realizing that food is meant to be fuel, not your friend.

Hear me again: *food is not your friend*. It's just fuel to move your body from point A to point B. And food is not your enemy. It's just stuff, over there in the kitchen, that's going to be part of the guarantee that you are going to have the strength to live life for Christ tomorrow.

I love Taco Bell. I just do. I mean, where else can you get an eighty-nine-cent burrito? Nowhere, I dare say. Nowhere. Today, as I was headed on a three-hour road trip, I stopped and purchased a burrito and a small diet Mountain Dew. About one-third of the way through the burrito, when I had a bite that perfectly combined the beans, the red sauce, the onions, and the stringy cheese, I sighed and thought, "I hope there's a Taco Bell in heaven." Seriously. I thought that. How weird.

But I do wonder if there will be food in heaven. Look at

Adam and Eve—they ate before the fall, so food wasn't something that entered the world along with sin. And in Revelation 19, it talks about the wedding feast that God is preparing for us. The word *feast* means one thing to me: *lots of food.* I have no idea (because the Bible doesn't say) what the food will be like or what our eating habits will be, but I think there is something beautiful and glorious about well-made food with fresh ingredients. God displays His beauty in His creation, and that includes fruits and vegetables.

He made your stomach to want food. So eat it. Just make healthy choices. Ask God, at every meal, to guide you. It's part of His promise in Psalm 23:3:

> He guides me along the right paths for his name's sake.

So just ask. Here's a sample of what I pray, in my mind, before each meal:

> *Hey, God. Thanks so much for this food. I appreciate You providing it for me. I want to glorify You with my body, so I'd love some help knowing what to order and when to stop eating. Thanks. Love You.*

Simple, right? Kind of silly, maybe. But it works. God loves to answer our prayers, especially when it comes to how to express our love for Him. The honest truth about this whole stomach thing? You are going to have to work at this and pray about it. The other honest truth? No one will ever know. This isn't something you're going to be chastised or celebrated for. This is a higher level of holy, a deeper challenge to know the

Lord. This is an inward struggle with an inward solution. God is cheering for you and I am cheering for you, but other than that, no one is going to know unless you let him or her into this area of your life. Whether you are skinny or fat or short or tall, whether food is an issue for you or just another part of your day, you still have to choose to love God the most and offer your body to Him as a living sacrifice (Romans 12:1).

We were meant to hunger for food. We were meant to thirst for a drink. Our bodies reflect our spirits—what happens on the outside is meant to reflect the inside. Your body experiences hunger and thirst because your soul does too. When we feel our insides hungering, thirsting, longing for God, He always fills us! Just read Matthew 5:6:

> Blessed are those who hunger and thirst for righteousness,
> for they will be filled.

Do you know that feeling? The feeling that something is missing in your heart? That your emotional or spiritual gas tank is close to, or running on, empty? I do too. That's when I realize that I am made to hunger after God. He is able to fill me—all the things my spirit needs are found in Jesus. Think this one through, and use your journal to record times when you feel empty and in need of more of God. Then share with your small group, fill up by reading the Word and spending time in worship, and let God satisfy you.

(And just because you've been such a champ and have made it this far, I've added my favorite salsa recipe in the appendix. Enjoy!)

chew on this

Ponder:

How are you feeling about this chapter?

How do you relate to it? What struggles have you faced with food?

What's your favorite snack?

Read: Psalm 63:5; Psalm 78:30; Psalm 146:7

Look up: *food, eat, stomach, feed*

Do it:

Wait until you're hungry before eating. Then eat something beautiful and healthy. Then when you're full, stop eating. Make this your lifestyle.

chapter 10

Knees

I haven't had good knees since the midnineties. I played soccer the entire time I was growing up, and somehow my knees always took the brunt of the injuries. I remember specifically one time when I was going to kick the ball at the exact same moment that the girl on the other team was planning to kick it. We both used the inside of our right foot, and I kicked with all the gusto I could muster. Three hours later, I was in the doctor's office getting a knee brace because I had torn my meniscus disc. Nice.

The worst knee injury I ever received was when I was twenty. And I will tell you that to this day I haven't returned to a ski slope because of it. I went skiing in West Virginia with a big group of students from my youth group. The kids were all excited, I was all excited; it was an exciting trip. I actually had never even been skiing before, so I was really looking forward to it.

The first day I took the little ski class and did fine. Bunny slopes were my style, and I was getting a grip on how to slow down and stop. Don't get me wrong, I wasn't a "good" skier by any means, and the ski instructor made sure I knew that. He said at no time would it be a good idea for me to be alone. He added I didn't have the natural abilities to ski, and I probably wasn't going to enjoy it. "Well, thank you very much, sir. That was really kind of you." I had already paid for a two-day pass and bought a supercute new jacket, so whether he liked it or not, I was determined to be out there doing my best to look cool for the students and any cute boys I might come in contact with. And by "contact," I meant probably landing on them when I fell or slamming into them at high rates of speed because I was completely out of control.

When ski school was over, the students in the youth group were waiting on me. Jake said, "Annie, follow us to this slope. It'll be easy for you." I looked at the sign and saw a big black diamond. Since I had never been skiing before, I had no idea what the signs meant.

Just in case you're like me, let me inform you: a green circle is for beginners (that would be me), and a blue square is for intermediate skiers (that was not me), and a black diamond is for expert skiers (that definitely wasn't me).

Well, before I could say "Save me, bunny slope," I was at the top of the black diamond, following the students from our youth group down the hill. I figured if they thought I could ski it, I probably could. We were all wrong. Very, very wrong.

I knew pretty quickly that black diamond must mean death for beginners, because I was going down the mountain super-quick and I couldn't stop myself. I realized within about one hundred seconds that I was in a bad situation and I needed to find a means of exit. Then I saw, right in front of our condos, a snow-blowing machine. At the base of the machine I noticed what looked like a huge pile of snow. So as I turned the corner, I thought to myself, "Just land in that huge pile of snow and you'll be fine."

I skied toward it, and my right ski slammed straight through the pile and got stuck. Because it wasn't snow. It was ice. My left ski, on the other hand, remained unstuck, and so continued flying forward. So what actually happened is that my entire body kept skiing really fast and left my right foot behind. Thus tearing my MCL, a rather important ligament in the knee. Which is not a fun injury to deal with on a twelve-hour bus ride home.

So though many of my friends are awesome skiers, and though I do really love cold weather, I do not ski. I will go to the resort and chill and look all snuggly in a warm outfit, but I've embraced the fact that my day (yes, only one day) on the slopes has come and gone.

If you learn anything from this, learn what those signs on the ski slopes mean. Because it could save your life. Or your knees.

Poor knees.

When it comes to how to worship God with our knees, it isn't as easy to classify as your mouth or your eyes. It's not like our knees are going to gossip. I mean, I don't think that's possible. But it's still totally possible for our knees to be instruments of righteousness. Below are a couple of different ways.

Kneel in Prayer

As has been the case every page of this book, I am *not* the total expert on any of these topics. I have so much room for improvement it isn't even funny. But I know this: when I run to God, with a prayer deep in my soul longing to get out, and I fall on my knees, He is always right there. Does He always answer my prayers in the exact way I want? Absolutely not. But He does always answer in the perfect way, at the perfect time.

I actually remember the first time I knelt to pray. It was when I accepted Christ as a five-year-old. I remember placing my little knees on the soft red velvet of the altar. I knew at the time that I was giving something away. I knew something was changing, and I knew in my heart that Jesus really died for me.

As a third grader, I knelt beside my bed the afternoon of our church's play. I was in a minor starring role that night, and downstairs my mother lay in bed with a migraine headache that was going to prevent her from coming to the show. I prayed as hard as a nine-year-old knows how that she would be healed and be able to come see the play. She was and she did.

As a twenty-three-year-old school teacher, I knelt in my kitchen and wept as I prayed for the Lord to step into a sad situation. One of my students was losing his father to cancer and it was breaking my heart. So I begged and pleaded that God would save the father and heal him. He died the next day, during our class's Christmas party.

Kneeling to pray shows an added layer of desperation. A deep need for God to intercede, to step into the situation and change things. When you pray from our knees, it also shows we understand who is in charge.

My youth minister, Michael, used to tell the story of one of his mentors, Dennis. A Scottish man, Dennis started every morning exactly the same way—sliding out of bed immediately onto the floor. Landing on his knees, he would pray to God and offer that day to Him. In fact, when Michael visited Dennis at his house, Michael saw the proof with his own eyes—two roundish spots on the carpet beside the bed, rubbed raw and bare from the daily kneeling. That, in my eyes, is a serious man of God. Daily kneeling, giving God control over his day and his life.

I love in Acts 9, when Peter knelt to pray. A wonderful woman, Tabitha, had died. All the women of the town were crying and mourning and showing Peter the beautiful things Tabitha had sewn for them.

> Peter sent them all out of the room; then he got down on his knees and prayed. Turning toward the dead woman, he said, "Tabitha, get up." She opened her eyes, and seeing Peter she sat up (verse 40).

We don't know what Peter prayed, but we know that he felt

it important to pray from a kneeling position. And God heard his prayers and brought Tabitha back to life. Peter took time to show with his body that he knew God was in control and more than capable of handling the situation.

I try to make it a habit to often kneel when I pray. I want to express with my body, with my knees, that God is the center of my universe and that He is the one I turn to when I am in need. There isn't some magical position that gets all your prayers answered; kneeling isn't going to guarantee that your friend will get saved or that your parent will be healed or that you'll get a car for Christmas. What kneeling in prayer says is that you are aware of your place in the big picture. And in that big picture, you know that God is in control, a King on His throne, and you trust His judgment.

I moved to Nashville on a Sunday afternoon. That morning at my home church, I cried the entire way through worship and sniffled through the sermon. At the end of the service, during a time of ministry, I went to the front of the sanctuary, off to one side, and got down on my knees. Tissues covering my eyes, I wept. I kept saying, "God, I can't do this. I can't leave my friends and family. I'm scared. I can't believe we're actually going through with this today." Things like that, over and over for about ten minutes.

Did it change the situation? Nope. I still packed my car and drove three and a half hours north that day. My mouth was asking some hard questions and begging God to rescue me from this hard change that was coming. *But* … my body was in a posture that let God know (and let me know) that in the end, I was still submitted to His will. My voice might have been shaky with doubt, but my knees were bent in total trust and submission to the one who really is in charge.

Does God need a reminder that He is the Boss? Nope. You do. I do. We all do. Sometimes it's easy for me to get in the flow of my days and forget to put God at the start and as the focus. Kneeling to pray, first thing in the morning, reminds me that I am the servant to a loving King and my life belongs to Him.

Kneel in Gratitude

In 1 Kings 8, King Solomon brought the ark of the covenant into the newly built temple. The ark was the place where God's presence rested. Think about it: God's presence actually *lived* in the ark. Now, because of Jesus, God's presence lives in each believer through the Holy Spirit, so nothing can separate us from Him. Until the temple was built, however, the ark had been kept in a tent, or tabernacle, and had even been stolen by the Philistines in King David's time (2 Samuel 6). Without the ark, the people couldn't be in God's presence. But now that Solomon had built a permanent home for God, His presence and protection would remain over Jerusalem. And as God's presence fills the temple, King Solomon begins to pray.

Starting at verse 22, we see the king standing in front of the assembly and praying. And for the next thirty verses, Solomon prayed beautifully to the Lord. When you read the whole prayer (and please read the whole prayer), you will almost feel like you're eavesdropping on a personal conversation. Solomon spoke to God like they were close, as if God was right there. And He was.

In verse 54, it says,

> When Solomon had finished all these prayers and supplications to the LORD, he rose from before the altar of the LORD, where he had been kneeling with his hands spread out toward heaven.

Here's the interesting part: in verse 22 Solomon was standing, and by verse 54, he was kneeling. Why? What are your thoughts on that? What happened in those few paragraphs, a prayer that lasted probably five minutes, that caused Solomon to fall on his knees? Picturing this moment in my head is so dramatic and beautiful to me—that as King Solomon went deeper and deeper into his prayer of thanks and gratitude, he couldn't remain standing. Maybe he slowly started bending over a little bit, overwhelmed by emotion. Then he put one knee on the ground and leaned on the other while he prayed. And as the people watched, he went from that stance to both knees on the ground, hands raised up toward heaven. Oh, how beautiful that must have been to see! A king, the strongest man in the country, slowly bowing down in gratitude to the King of kings.

Sometimes the deepest prayers of our hearts are best expressed if we're eighteen inches closer to the ground. Kneeling while praying in gratitude indicates honor, power, and respect to the one who is receiving our prayers.

I have also found myself kneeling in gratitude, picturing myself at the foot of a King who has given me the world. That's the God I know. Because He has forgiven my sins, blessed me with life and breath and friends and family, and provided everything I need, I just have to tell Him how grateful I am by kneeling before Him in prayer.

During worship, there are times when I just want to kneel down and say thanks. I find it really powerful for my heart and mind if I say thank you to God while I'm on my knees. Of course, this isn't the only way to express gratitude or to say thanks to God in a meaningful way. But it's a great way to do it.

I don't know if you know, but you have *a lot* to be grateful for. James 1:17 says,

> Every good and perfect gift is from above, coming down from the Father of the heavenly lights, who does not change like shifting shadows.

So everything you have, from your health to your friendships to a roof over your head to the food in your belly, is a gift from God. And we even have something else to be thankful for: that God doesn't change! I love that about Him.

Psalm 95:6 tells us to bow down to God in worship, after listing some of God's greatest attributes. Pretty much worshiping God and being thankful to Him go hand in hand, because isn't that what we're saying in worship? "Thank You, God, for being You. For loving us and taking care of us and sending Your Son to die on our behalf."

Take a few minutes to make up a list of the top ten things you're thankful for. (Flip back to the appendix to see my current Top Ten list.) After you write your list, kneel down in prayer and thank God for these ten things, and any others that come to mind. 'Cause once you start listing things you're thankful for, it's kind of hard to stop. And that's a good thing.

Kneel for Forgiveness

Sometimes you need to get on your knees because of your sin. Oh, girls, I have done it before. Struggling through sin is ugly, and there are times when temptation seems to be too much and you fall. At least, I do. And I feel so much shame that I have to come to God on my knees and ask for forgiveness, like the sinner I am.

In the Bible, Ezra dealt with this exact thing. In Ezra 9, when he heard of the sins of his people (Ezra 9), he had some strong physical reactions—tearing his clothes, pulling hair from his head and beard, and literally falling on the floor. And sitting there all day. It says in verse 3 that he was "appalled." The Hebrew word there is *shamem*, meaning "stunned, appalled in horror, devastated," even "deflowered." So it isn't a weak word.

Have you ever sinned in a way that appalled you? The kind of sin that makes you want to absolutely throw up and just be disgusted with yourself. I know I have. Or maybe you've seen someone else suffer from a sin, and your body wants to respond like that. Sin is horrible, huh? Deflowering. For sure.

In Ezra 9:5–6, when Ezra was finally able to recover a bit, look at what he did:

> Then, at the evening sacrifice, I rose from my self-abasement, with my tunic and cloak torn, and fell on my

173

> knees with my hands spread out to the Lord my God and prayed.

He fell on his knees and then prayed for his people, who were deep into sin. So he wasn't even the one who had sinned, but he was repenting. On his knees. Are you there? Can you think of a sinful area of your life where you just really need to get on your knees and ask God to forgive you? It's a horrible feeling, but the freedom of forgiveness is totally worth it.

When I was in high school, we had an evening service at church. The same group of people came every time—you know how that goes. We would have a time of worship, a time of teaching, and then a time of ministry. One night, our pastor told us a story that has never left me.

A man attended an evening service, much like ours, and week after week when ministry time began, he would slowly make laps around the sanctuary. *On his knees.* High school Annie would have found that really distracting and weird. What in the world was he doing?

One week, the pastor finally asked him about this behavior. After the service concluded, the pastor simply said, "Can you tell me what that is all about?" The man replied, "If you knew what God did for me, and if you knew what he had forgiven me for, you would understand."

That's a man who understood kneeling in forgiveness.

Kneel Because He Is Worthy

Scripture repeats this phrase over and over again: *Every knee shall bow*. Everyone is going to kneel. The Bible promises it. Look at Isaiah 45:23. Before Jesus was even on the scene, God told Isaiah that every knee was going to bow.

And in Philippians 2:10–11, it says

> that at the name of Jesus every knee should bow, in heaven and on earth and under the earth, and every tongue acknowledge that Jesus Christ is Lord, to the glory of God the Father.

At some point, *every* knee is going to bow before God. Even the people who here on earth are choosing to stand up and tell God who is boss—they will kneel. Even the people who claim God isn't real—they will kneel. And the ones who have served Him every single day—they will kneel. Isn't that an amazing thought?

Let's shrink it down. Imagine that you are in a football stadium getting ready to watch a game. You and eighty thousand of your closest friends are all standing and clapping, prepared for the team to walk onto the field. What if when the head coach comes out, instead of cheering, everyone gets down on their knees and bows? Wouldn't that be crazy to see? Every last person on their knees. Now multiply that by a million, and that will give you an idea of what it will look like when every knee bows. Except it won't be a head coach. It will be Jesus. For real. And that will be awesome.

But we have the choice now. We don't have to wait. We can

bow before God in our times of prayer or worship and express to Him today what everyone will say to Him one day—that He is our King and He is worthy.

So it's possible to make your knees instruments of righteousness. And even more than possible, it's really easy. You can do it today.

I ran across these verses from Ephesians today and decided I would get down on my knees, just like Paul did when he wrote it, and pray for you. And I pray that once you've read these verses, you'll kneel down and pray for some people you love too.

For this reason I kneel before the Father, from whom every family in heaven and on earth derives its name. I pray that out of his glorious riches he may strengthen you with power through his Spirit in your inner being, so that Christ may dwell in your hearts through faith. And I pray that you, being rooted and established in love, may have power, together with all the Lord's holy people, to grasp how wide and long and high and deep is the love of Christ, and to know this love that surpasses knowledge—that you may be filled to the measure of all the fullness of God.

Now to him who is able to do immeasurably more than all we ask or imagine, according to his power that is at work within us, to him be glory in the church and in Christ Jesus throughout all generations, forever and ever! Amen.

Ephesians 3:14–21

Amen!

chew on this

Ponder:

What kinds of things are you praying about right now?

Read: Psalm 95; Ephesians 3

Look up: *knees, bow, kneel*

Do it:

Take time today to kneel down and pray.

Make a Top Ten list of the things for which you are grateful.

chapter 11

Feet

Oh, shoes. Seriously. Do we even have to talk about how much girls love shoes? Do you love shoes? Because I do. I'm not addicted; I'm not some high fashionista who pays hundreds of dollars for a pair of pumps that I wear once. But I will pay one hundred dollars for a pair of Steve Madden tan leather boots and wear them every other day because I totally have a crush on them. For me, the winter is boots and the summer is flip-flops. The spring and fall I get stumped every year. But you can bet your money that by September 1, I've got a serious flip-flop tan that doesn't go away until the New Year rolls around. Because these little piggies love to be free all summer long.

I sort of love my feet. Unlike my sausage fingers, my toes are pretty well shaped, and believe it or not, I don't bite my toenails. (That is sick and wrong.) I love getting pedicures, and in fact, I'm hoping to get one this week, and I'm seriously considering a bright-yellow polish color. I've wanted it for a while, but my friends have peer-pressured me away from it the last few times, encouraging other shades, like various pinks. But I can't really resist the urge for yellow anymore.

My friend Meredith recently ran a marathon. She had trained for months and was as physically ready as one could possibly be. (Read: she's a total champ.) And when the day arrived, she ran the race, finished, and actually survived the 26.2 miles, which amazes me. Her only mistake? She didn't trim her toenails. Weird, right? I mean, of all the details to forget, that one is bizarre, but costly. Because within a month, both of her big toenails fell off. Completely.

Apparently when you run 26.2 miles and your toenails crunch into the front of your shoes thousands of times, they can't really survive the impact. Within a few weeks, they give up and fall off. Poor toenails.

As Meredith sat on her mom's couch, feet aching and big toes nail-less, her mom made some great points. "Mere, you have to take care of your feet," she said, "because you only get two. They are very complex—lots of bones, muscles, and tendons. If your feet don't work, you can't go where you want to go in life."

When Meredith's roommate ran a half marathon, Meredith taped pictures of her injured big toes to her roommate's door. She hoped that this would be a motivation and reminder for her roommate to make the necessary trims before the race.

Good reminder, right? And actually, Meredith offered the photos for you to see, but I kindly and quickly said no thanks.

So we're going to talk about taking care of your feet and your feet taking you places. Where? How? What does that look like?

And I'm sure you're not surprised that I'm taking this opportunity to talk about shoes.

Lead with Your Tennies

I used to wear tennis shoes all the time. As a soccer player, and a tomboy, they were the shoes I always picked. Tennis shoes are always a safe choice—they stay in place (unlike flip-flops, which can flip here or flop there), they're comfortable (unlike heels), and they last for quite a while. Actually, now that I'm thinking it through, I still really love them.

Tennies allow us to do some amazing things with our feet, but one of the truest ways to glorify God with your feet is to lead. Lead people to Christ. Lead people away from sin. Lead people by the way you live. At the University of Georgia, there is a place called the Tate Center, which in my time was where everyone hung out. (Remember the tripping spot? At Tate.) Throughout my college days, people would come and "preach" at the Tate Center. What that consisted of was huge signs saying "YOU ARE SINNERS GOING TO HELL," and men and women yelling at us with the loudest voices they could muster. It was, in a word, ridiculous. I remember watching them one day and thinking how ineffective they were sharing the gospel. And sadly, they were carrying the same Bible I was, living life in front of these students and calling it "Christianity"—just like I was doing on a day-to-day basis. It made me sick.

You know in your heart that people like that didn't lead you to Christ. Though it does get conversations going and give Christians a lot of open doors in class and on campus, those aren't the kinds of leaders that draw people into a love relationship with Jesus.

Instead, we lead people to Christ by living before them a life that seeks to glorify God. Are you allowed to make mistakes? Of course! This was one of the most difficult stumbling blocks for me in high school and part of college. I believed that the best way for my friends to see Christ in me was for me to live "perfectly" in front of them. So that meant I didn't express any hurt feelings, I always was smiley and in a good mood, I never told the truth about making mistakes, and I didn't ask the types of questions that lacked concrete answers. I thought that being a leader for Christ meant avoiding all things messy— no one needed to see me struggle or hurt or question. But Philippians 2:12 says that being a Christian means working out your salvation:

> Therefore, my dear friends, as you have always obeyed— not only in my presence, but now much more in my absence—continue to work out your salvation with fear and trembling.

To "work out your salvation" means to not have all the answers and to not be enslaved to perfection. Remember in the

"Hands" chapter when I talked about that missions trip I led? Well, one of the biggest problems with that whole trip for me was that I spent the majority of the time trying to be perfect. I couldn't get past the idea that being a good leader meant being perfect. And let me tell you, it's quite hard to hide your imperfections when you're sharing a room with seven other girls and sharing a house with twenty people and having only sleep time and shower time to yourself. Like a Coke bottle that has been shaken up, when the pressure got to be too much, I just exploded. Instead of my imperfections trickling out like a leaky faucet, I was a rushing river of issues. Not pretty, people. Not pretty.

I say all this to remind you that being a leader doesn't mean your sneakers have to stay brilliantly clean. Leading your friends to Christ, or just leading your Christian friends in life choices, is going to be messy. You are going to make mistakes, bad things are going to happen to good people, and you're going to have to trust God anyway. Life is messy. Life is unfair. But that doesn't mean you can't be a leader for your friends, family, team, or church. Remember 1 Timothy 4:12:

> Don't let anyone look down on you because you are young, but set an example for the believers in speech, in life, in love, in faith and in purity.

Set an example. How? By being an orchestra of instruments of righteousness. Live in such a way that your life tells the world that you are working out your salvation.

Go in Galoshes

One of my favorite scriptures in the Bible talks about feet. It is Isaiah 52:7:

> How beautiful on the mountains are the feet of those who bring good news, who proclaim peace, who bring good tidings, who proclaim salvation, who say to Zion, "Your God reigns!"

How beautiful are our feet! God calls us, throughout the Bible, to spread word of His love and His Son to all the nations. All the people. All the cities. Paris, France; Ciudad Cortez, Costa Rica; Hoschton, Georgia; Chicago, Illinois; Vancouver, British Columbia; London, England; Beijing, China; Jackson Hole, Wyoming.

We could go on forever listing cities and countries on this planet. There are hundreds of countries and millions of cities. How many have you been to? I can already tell you the answer—not enough! The world is huge. There are so many different places that it would be virtually impossible to list them all. As you know from where you live, different areas divide up your town. For example, I used to live in Atlanta, Georgia. Well, I actually lived in Marietta. But more specifically, I lived in Kennesaw. Whew. See what I mean? I'm sure you could list the divisions in your state too. And so could the twentysomething girl sitting at her computer tonight in Paris, France. Actually, she's in Jouy-en-Josas.

So, all that silliness to remind you that the world is big. And yet it's tiny. You can make any city as big and unfriendly as you want or as small and intimate as you want. But you'll never know that if you sit in your rooms in your homes in your city.

Living in every city on earth are people. Girls like you. Guys like your brother. Parents like your best friend's. Teachers like the one who gave you an A in chemistry even when you probably didn't deserve it. Almost seven billion people live on the earth right now. Every day, about 350,000 babies are born. That's about half the population of the whole state of South Dakota. That's a lot of people. All these people, every single one of them, have a name. A face. A heart that needs to hear the good news of the Gospel of Jesus Christ.

The last words Jesus said on earth before He ascended into heaven are found in Matthew 28:18–20:

> "All authority in heaven and on earth has been given to me. Therefore go and make disciples of all nations, baptizing them in the name of the Father and of the Son and of the Holy Spirit, and teaching them to obey everything I have commanded you."

Pretty much what Jesus was saying is get steppin'! Get out there and tell the world about Him. Make disciples of all nations. I like the idea of wearing galoshes when you go. Galoshes are nothing more than rubber rain boots (but to say "go in rubber rain boots" just doesn't have the same ring as "go in galoshes"). I love these kinds of boots because you can go anywhere in them. No weather is going to surprise you if you're galoshed out. Rain? Bring it. Snow? I don't fear you. Lightning storm? Made of rubber, baby. Sun? Perfect, 'cause they are cute too. So there is no mission field God can call you to where galoshes are a bad idea.

The Lord has been moving my feet to mission fields my whole life, though I'll admit I haven't worn galoshes in all these places.

When I was in seventh grade, our youth group went on a trip to downtown Atlanta, a twenty-five-minute drive in a fifteen-passenger van. We went to an inner-city nursing home for the afternoon. Brad, our youth director, asked each of us to find an older person to sit and talk with for a couple of hours. It was really awkward at first, but it ended up being interesting and moving to spend so much time with someone totally different from myself—him being an eighty-five-year-old black man and I being a twelve-year-old white girl. It was the shortest missions trip I've ever been on, but I know God led my feet there to be a friend to that man, even if just for a day.

When I was a senior in high school, I went on a missions trip to Tennessee. Yes, I lived in Georgia, and yes, Tennessee is right next door. But there are areas of Tennessee (and every other state) that are very poor and need missions work to be done there. The places my feet took me that week will never leave my memory. We went to one house where a mom with seven children lived. None of them knew how to read (including the mom). They drank water and made us lemonade from a puddle where the dog was standing. They slept on chairs in a house with no doors or windows. They couldn't go to school because the bus wasn't able to drive up the mountain and the car didn't ever have any gas. It was absolutely unbelievable. And what did we do? Not much—played with the kids, cleared some trash out of her yard, and repaired her porch. But the sight of that woman crying as we left, thanking us so much for even coming over to see her, forever changed me. And it's not like this happened in India or Africa or somewhere desolate and foreign. This happened here. In our country.

I love doing missions work in the United States. There is something really powerful about ministering to the people in my own culture who speak my own language. Whether it's teens in Lake Placid, New York, or college students at the University of Kentucky, or hurricane victims in New Orleans, it's important that our feet lead us to serve our own people sometimes.

But just like Jesus said in Matthew, He wants us to go to all the nations, and I've loved the chances I've had to go on missions trips to other countries. I've helped to build churches and homes in Cortez, Costa Rica, where the children showed up in droves for vacation Bible school, and it was so hot that I started sweating before I even finished showering. I've performed on stages all around greater Paris, France, singing and dancing and presenting the gospel. I've been a counselor at summer camps in Edinburgh, Scotland, where my friend Harry always makes me a serving of the most delicious egg salad. I've sat cross-legged on the floor of an orphanage in Accra, Ghana, and fed tiny babies milk from a spoon. For those few minutes, I didn't feel the heat of Africa, only the cool of the cement floors and the softness of the babies in my arms. Sometimes sharing the gospel looks like that.

As you know, I live in Nashville, Tennessee. Not a commonly listed place on missions-trip applications, but definitely a mission field. Even if you're a famous songwriter or a Tennessee Titan or a starving artist, you need Jesus. So God brings people to Nashville to live as missionaries. And He calls people to Washington, D.C., and Los Angeles, California, and Waco, Texas, and every small town in the world.

Because, honestly, wherever God takes you—schools, cities, countries, friends' homes—those become mission fields for you. How beautiful are the feet that bring good news, right? Wherever you go, you bring good news. And a cute pair of galoshes, just in case it rains.

Serve in Sandals

Let your feet take you to places where you can serve. And you may not love to hear this, but in a lot of cases, those places are down the hall or up the stairs in your own home. We have to love serving the people in our own little bubbles before we can love the people outside our bubbles.

I'll tell you a secret. And if this gets out, I'll know exactly where it came from. But I'm a pretty selfish person. There are some people on this earth who are natural servants. They immediately think of other people first, volunteer whenever possible, and somehow have a smile on their faces for most of it. If that's you, I congratulate you. (And I humbly request that you teach me how to be like you.) But that isn't me. I have to choose to work at and focus on caring about other people more than I care about myself.

Jesus set a beautiful example for us. (Well, in all things, really, but here we're just going to focus on how He served the people around Him.) His very first miracle, turning the water into wine, was an act of service for all the people at the wedding. I also think about when Jesus washed the feet of His disciples. The story is told in John 13:2–17. (I'm using *The Message* version because I like how it tells the story.)

> Just before the Passover Feast, Jesus knew that the time had come to leave this world to go to the Father. Having loved his dear companions, he continued to love them right to the end. It was suppertime. The Devil by now had Judas, son of Simon the Iscariot, firmly in his grip, all set for the betrayal.
>
> Jesus knew that the Father had put him in complete charge of everything, that he came from God and was on his way back to God. So he got up from the supper table, set aside his robe, and put on an apron. Then he poured water into a basin and began to wash the feet of the disciples, drying them with his apron. When he got to Simon Peter, Peter said, "Master, you wash my feet?"
>
> Jesus answered, "You don't understand now what I'm doing, but it will be clear enough to you later."
>
> Peter persisted, "You're not going to wash my feet—ever!"

Jesus said, "If I don't wash you, you can't be part of what I'm doing."

"Master!" said Peter. "Not only my feet, then. Wash my hands! Wash my head!"

Jesus said, "If you've had a bath in the morning, you only need your feet washed now and you're clean from head to toe. My concern, you understand, is holiness, not hygiene. So now you're clean. But not every one of you." (He knew who was betraying him. That's why he said, "Not every one of you.") After he had finished washing their feet, he took his robe, put it back on, and went back to his place at the table.

Then he said, "Do you understand what I have done to you? You address me as 'Teacher' and 'Master,' and rightly so. That is what I am. So if I, the Master and Teacher, washed your feet, you must now wash each other's feet. I've laid down a pattern for you. What I've done, you do. I'm only pointing out the obvious. A servant is not ranked above his master; an employee doesn't give orders to the employer. If you understand what I'm telling you, act like it—and live a blessed life."

So Jesus, the obvious leader in the situation, actually becomes the servant. He took time to care more about the other people in the room (His disciples) than He cared about Himself. Can you imagine how gross those feet were? The dudes had been wearing sandals and walking around outside for days—they probably had all manner of ick and yuck on their feet. And yet Jesus touched them, cleaned them, and showed us an example of how to serve.

But in our world, there really isn't that much opportunity to wash the feet of our friends. So it's not like we can really serve in that way. How, then, can we serve people today? Yesterday on my computer, I got a message that some friends were gathering to deliver blankets to homeless men and women in Nashville. The low last night was 2 degrees, so those folks definitely needed some sort of covering. I was unable to go—I already had a meeting—but what an easy, low-cost, low-commitment way to serve. Those kinds of chances are around you every day: giving blankets, socks, or towels to the homeless in your community via some homeless shelter or ministry; volunteering at your local boys or girls club. As you may recall, in Proverbs 31, it says that a godly wife "opens her arms to the poor" (verse 20). We are called to love the poor and the orphaned.

As a freshman in college, I had the opportunity to go on a missions trip to Long Beach, California, and work in a homeless shelter for a week. Not exactly what I pictured for my first college spring break, but it was one of those times when I had the chance to choose to love others more than myself—and I took it. It changed my outlook on homelessness forever. Because we slept in the places the homeless slept, we ate the same day-old bagels they ate, and we showered in the same little shower they used. And yes, it was gross, and yes, I smelled weird when I got back home. But even just in that one week of living like a homeless person, I saw the importance of loving and serving them. I'd listen to stories over dinner that broke my heart. Men and women (and children!) would spend hours just hanging out with us, as we folded the donated clothes and bleached the donated toys. Serving sometimes looks like that. Gross. Dirty. Unsanitary. Just like when Jesus washed those feet, twenty-four dirty, dusty feet, sometimes serving isn't a beautiful act that leaves us feeling all warm and fuzzy.

But we serve anyway. And in this day and time, nonprofit organizations are popping up everywhere that want you to help. They *need* you to help, whether you're looking to do something in your own town or state or as far away as the earth (and your parents) will allow you to go. (Check the appendix for some of the ministries that you can go to and help.)

In the long run, there is one main thing you need to remember: whether you're helping out an elderly neighbor by mowing her grass or washing the clothes of street kids in India, you were made to serve. Because of God's great love for us, we can love others. And Jesus told us to go into the world and share the good news about Him. The question isn't when, it's where. So take those feet, and some cute shoes, and start walking and talking. Let your feet lead you to what God has for you.

chew on this

Ponder:

List three mission fields that the Lord has given you.

1.

2.

3.

Read: Mark 6:11; John 13:1–17; Romans 10:14–15

Look up: *feet, walk, go*

Do it:

How can you use your feet as instruments of righteousness *today*?

Find one way to serve God and others today.

chapter 12

From Head to Foot

As I dried the five-year-old girl's hair, we stood in front of a tall mirror, her little body standing in front of mine. I was babysitting for her and her brother, and we were in those final crucial moments before they went to sleep. You know the ones I mean—the moments that never go quite quick enough.

"I'm skinny, aren't I?" the girl asked innocently. Placing her hands on her hips and pushing in, she said, "I think I'm skinny. But I used to think I was fat."

"Why would you think that?" I asked her. Because, seriously, five years old? Isn't that a little young to know the real difference between fat and skinny and use the derogatory tone at the appropriate time?

"I just don't want to be fat when I'm a grown-up. I want to be pretty."

Not skinny. Pretty.

And that reminded me of why we're on this journey together. Why you're taking time to read this book and I'm taking time to write it. Because the enemy of our hearts, the one who comes to steal, kill, and destroy, doesn't play fair. He doesn't respect the innocence of children or the recovery period for broken hearts. Satan is a cheater, a liar, and all around bad. Nothing is sacred to him, and he will inject his venom and lies at any moment possible.

So I think it's fair to say that I'm sad about that entire conversation, our culture, and our worldview of beauty. But on the other hand, isn't that the reason God has called us together? To fight through these lies and learn the truth and grasp what it means to glorify Him with our whole selves. From head to foot.

I also think it's superimportant, before we part ways, to give you an idea of the protection you have as a believer—the armor God has promised to cover the beautiful body He has given you .

Let's look at Ephesians 6:10–18 first, and then we'll dissect it a bit.

Finally, be strong in the Lord and in his mighty power. Put on the full armor of God, so that you can take your stand against the devil's schemes. For our struggle is not against flesh and blood, but against the rulers, against the authorities, against the powers of this dark world and against the spiritual forces of evil in the heavenly realms. Therefore put on the full armor of God, so that when the day of evil comes, you may be able to stand your ground, and after you have done everything, to stand. Stand firm then, with the belt of truth buckled around your waist, with the breastplate of righteousness in place, and with your feet fitted with the readiness that comes from the gospel of peace. In addition to all this, take up the shield of faith, with which you can extinguish all the flaming arrows of the evil one. Take the helmet of salvation and the sword of the Spirit, which is the word of God.

And pray in the Spirit on all occasions with all kinds of prayers and requests. With this in mind, be alert and always keep on praying for all the Lord's people.

The Belt of Truth

Truth is the anchor, and what holds all the other pieces of your defense in place. Without the belt of truth, without an understanding of what is true, then the rest may just fall apart. Truth is a binder—like the egg in meat loaf. You may not be able to taste it, but it's what holds everything else together. (Speaking of … If you want to make a meal to impress the family or friends, make Joe's Meat Loaf. The recipe is in the appendix.)

How do you put on the belt of truth? By filling your mind with truth. Is that sentence on repeat or what?? I know. But it's still true. You have to know truth to claim truth to wear truth. Use the Lie and Truth cards you made in chapter two to help you. Consider trying to memorize one Bible verse a month. Do something to get the truth into you. And then wear it, make it your own, and trust God's truth to anchor your armor.

The Breastplate of Righteousness

We are told in Ephesians that the covering meant to protect all your vital organs is to be made of righteousness. So all these choices you're making with your eyes, ears, hands, feet, all of it—are all working for your advantage to be your protection. Your righteousness, or attempt at it (let's be honest), is protecting you, guarding your most vital organs, which include your heart and your stomach, as we've already discussed. So next time the righteousness choice seems like a hard choice, just remember this: by following God's lead toward the right decision, you are actually strengthening your armor.

Feet Fitted with the Readiness from the Gospel of Peace

Honestly, wherever you are today, God has placed you there, and you have a hope to share. Being ready to share that hope is part of your armor—part of your protection. If I choose to remember things about God that are true, and things about the gospel, then my feet can lead me anywhere without fear. God is for me, who can be against me (Romans 8:31)? Just like with the breastplate thing, when you're willing to share the gospel, and have your feet covered in that readiness, you are protected. Your sweet little feet, which are leading you everywhere God is directing you to go, are safe for the next journey. Get ready to share about God; pray for opportunities to show that your feet are covered. And then talk—about God, about grace, about how your life is different because God busted into your world and rescued you from sin.

The Shield of Faith

I love how Hebrews 11:1 starts by saying "faith is being ..." Because I think they are so true, and it's a great way to look at things. Faith is just being. Faith is a way to live, a way to be, and not just something you do. It's something you are. Ask God to fill you with faith—faith in Him, faith in His promises, faith in His ways. And then use the assurance that you feel well up in your heart to fight off the lies. Hold it up as a shield. Meant to protect you from the arrows of the enemy, it is the shield that you hold over your heart. My friend Matt Wertz has a great song called "Keep Faith," and my favorite lines say,

> *If there is anything that I'm sure of*
> *I know that we were made for love*
> *So if you start to break*
> *Keep faith.*

That's exactly what the shield is all about. Be sure of this: you were made for love; you were made for God's love. So even if you start to break ... well, you know the rest.

The Helmet of Salvation

The purpose of a helmet is to keep your head safe. Because your brain can't exactly be replaced. In the armor of God, that helmet is made of your salvation. Possibly the strongest thing you have is your assurance that by Jesus dying on the cross, you have been saved from your sin. Knowing that, believing that, is what protects your mind from the doubts that Satan would like you to believe. I don't question my salvation often, but I do know that I need my mind to be protected. So many lies try to come into my mind that I find myself depending on the helmet of salvation to save me from them! I believe that Jesus is all about rescuing us, anytime and anywhere.

The Sword of the Spirit

The sword of the Spirit, it says in Ephesians, is the Word of God. Plain and simple, it's the Bible. In all the armor that God offers us in these verses, this is the only weapon you have that is offensive, meaning that this is the only piece you can use to wage war. What does it look like to wield the sword of the Spirit? Use the Lie and Truth cards you made earlier! When you start to see the battle coming (remember that is part of using our minds for the glory of God—N = Notice the Patterns!), get those cards out and *fight*, y'all. *Fight*! Read those scriptures out loud until you believe them. Say them over and over again until something in you thinks they may actually be true. It gets easier with time, just like training with a real sword does. At first, the sword is heavy and exhausting and awkward, but the longer the knight uses it, the more it becomes almost a natural extension of his arm. So it is with your Bible. Don't have a Bible? Let your youth-group leader know, let your youth pastor know, or let me know.

Dress for Success

My friend Nan taught me something pretty cool when I was in high school. Years later, I'm still doing it. Every morning when I'm in the shower, I review the pieces of the armor of God. I remind myself what they are and how they'll affect me that day. It's like a combination of prayer and repetition. I take time each day to talk with God about the different pieces of armor, specifically if something is going on that involves one piece directly. For example, when I'm headed out on a missions trip, I find myself often thinking about my feet being "fitted with the readiness that comes from the gospel of peace." Or if I have to make an ethical decision, I think about the breastplate of righteousness and talk things over with God. I mean, besides getting clean, what else are you doing in the shower? Why not take time to get spiritually dressed, right?

So there you have it. We've been hanging out awhile, and we've come to the end of the road for now. I'm praying for you today. Praying that the things you've read and learned in these chapters, information and embarrassing stories from a very flawed storyteller, have somehow helped you fall more in love with God. I pray that in the next few weeks, months, and years, you'll see your life continue to be molded and shaped into what God has planned for you. Somehow I really think you're going to be a part of the change in our generation. You, choosing to live holy and righteous lives and be different on the inside, are the one who will make a difference on the outside—in your neighborhood and around the world.

But don't quit on this book yet. Go back and reread the things you've underlined. Make some of the recipes and read over your cards. Hang the armor of God somewhere you'll easily see it. Every day, seek to be more like Jesus. From head to foot.

chew on this

Ponder:

How can you picture the armor of God helping you out on a daily basis?

Can you think of a specific time when you needed to put on the full armor of God?

Which piece of the armor do you feel is most useful to you today?

Which piece do you want to get better at using?

Read: Ephesians 6

Look up: *armor, protect, shield, sword, faith*

Do it:

Now that you've finished the book, how are you different?

Which chapters meant the most to you? Why?

Which chapters did you relate to the most?

Go back and read what you connected with, or even highlighted, in the book.

Appendix

Introduction

Amazing Onion Soup

Ingredients

- 8 onions, sliced
- 2 cloves garlic, minced
- 1/3 cup olive oil
- 2 tablespoons all-purpose flour
- 8 cups beef stock
- 1/4 cup dry white wine
- 1/2 teaspoon dried thyme
- 1 bay leaf

- salt and pepper
- 1 loaf french bread
- 2 cups grated Gruyère cheese

Directions

Sauté onions and garlic in oil over low heat until tender and golden yellow. Sprinkle flour over onions, then cook a few minutes more, browning the flour well. Add stock and wine and bring to a boil, then add thyme and bay leaf. Reduce heat, cover, and simmer gently for 20 minutes or so. Add salt and pepper to taste.

Meanwhile, slice french bread into 3/4-inch slices and butter both sides. Toast slices on griddle until golden brown. Ladle soup into an ovenproof bowl, add toasted bread, and cover with cheese. Place ovenproof bowl on a baking sheet lined with tinfoil. Bake in the oven at 350 degrees Fahrenheit or 5 minutes under a hot broiler.

Chapter 4

Sweet-Potato Fries

This is my friend Jason's recipe, so please call them "Jason's Fries." (He will totally blush.)

Ingredients

- 2 sweet potatoes
- 1 tablespoon of olive oil

- salt and pepper, to taste
- cinnamon, to taste
- sugar, to taste

Directions

Slice sweet potatoes into strips—or rounds, if you prefer. Then toss them in olive oil, salt, fresh-cracked black pepper, a little cinnamon, and a little sugar. Bake them in the oven at 400 degrees for about 30 minutes. (This will make enough for two people.)

Musicians Not to Miss

These are Christian artists who may or may not play Christian music. But you can trust that the lyrics won't be loaded with cuss words.

- Dave Barnes
- Matt Wertz
- Ellie Holcomb
- Brooke Fraser
- Andrew Ripp
- Tara-Leigh Cobble
- Andrew Peterson
- Ben Rector
- Drew Holcomb and the Neighbors
- Steve Moakler

Chapter 6

Puppy Chow

Ingredients

- 1/2 cup peanut butter
- 1/4 cup butter
- 1 cup chocolate chips
- ½ teaspoon vanilla
- 9 cups Crispix cereal (any flavor)
- 1 ½ cups powdered sugar

Directions

Combine peanut butter, butter, and chocolate chips in a micro-wave-safe bowl. Microwave for one minute, then stir to blend all ingredients thoroughly. Add 1/2 teaspoon vanilla. Stir well. Place the 9 cups of Crispix cereal in a very large bowl. Pour the peanut butter–chocolate mixture over the cereal and toss evenly, making sure all the cereal gets a good coating. Cover with powdered sugar, sprinkling evenly over the cereal and tossing as you sprinkle to coat each piece well.

Chapter 9

Waffles with Peanut Butter

Here's my tip for making waffles with peanut butter: Put the waffle in a toaster oven and get it a little crispy. Pull it out, put peanut butter on it (chunky is my preference), and then put it back in the toaster oven. But stay close, because the peanut butter can burn! Stand there and watch until the peanut butter starts to turn a little dark brown. Then pull out the waffle and enjoy. But listen, it is *really* not fun to get a peanut-butter burn on the roof of your mouth, so proceed with caution. As your mama told you when you were a kid, blow on it before you eat.

Websites for Help with Anorexia and/or Bulimia

- Remuda Ranch:
  www.remudaranch.com/resourcesArticles.aspx

- National Eating Disorders Association:
  www.nationaleatingdisorders.org

Avocado-Feta Salsa

Okay, this is my very favorite salsa recipe. You can put it on chicken or in tacos, or just eat it with chips. And depending on the season, you may want to leave out the avocado. Since I'm cooking for one, and this makes enough for four, I usually don't use the avocado—so the salsa will last longer in the fridge. But if you're making salsa for a party, use the avocado—it's delicious. (And I think I've officially over-explained at this point.)

Ingredients

- 4 plum tomatoes, chopped
- 2 tablespoons finely chopped red onion
- 2 garlic cloves, minced
- 1 (4-ounce) package crumbled feta cheese

- 1 tablespoon chopped fresh parsley
- 3 tablespoons red-wine vinegar
- 2 tablespoons olive oil
- 1/2 teaspoon dried oregano
- 1/2 teaspoon salt
- 2 avocados, chopped (optional)

Directions

Stir together the first nine ingredients. Then gently stir in avocado just before serving.

Chapter 10

The Top Ten Things I'm Thankful for Today (In No Particular Order)

1. My parents

2. My health (my sprained ankle has finally healed!)

3. My friends in Atlanta

4. My friends in Nashville

5. The way the Lord has guided me recently

6. The way the Lord has provided for me (financially and relationally)

7. That my roommate and I found a new house to live in

8. That I totally love my job

9. The way the Lord has expressed His love for me through friends

10. The people in my life who pray for me on a daily basis

Chapter 11

Missions Opportunities

- Youth With a Mission: *www.ywam.org* (Locations worldwide!)

- The Mocha Club: *www.themochaclub.org* (Trips offered every year to different countries in Africa.)

- Adventures in Missions: *www.adventures.org* (Huge variety of trips offered, from short term to more than a year.)

Chapter 12

Joe's Meat Loaf

I know. Meat loaf is weird. Just trust me on this one, mmkay?

Ingredients

- 3 pounds lean ground beef
- 3 eggs, beaten (told ya they were important!)
- 1 cup Heinz 57 steak sauce
- 3 cups green onions, chopped

- 1 package dry onion-soup mix
- 2 stalks celery, chopped
- 2 cups Cheez-It crackers, crumbled
- 2 tablespoons chopped garlic
- 2 ounces red-wine vinegar
- 2 ounces light soy sauce
- 1 cup medium salsa
- salt, pepper, hot sauce (to taste)

Directions

Mix all ingredients together in a large bowl. Mold meat into two loaves and place in two medium-sized pans. Bake at 350 degrees for 1 hour, 15 minutes. Check for doneness (you'll know it's ready when the juices run clear).

Acknowledgments

I'm not going to make this short—like an acceptance speech at the Grammys, you just never know if you'll ever be on this stage again. So I'm going to say everything I want to say, even if the music starts playing.

To the amazing blog community, those who write alongside me (my blogmies) and those who read along (my bloggites), and to my other readers and friends from places like (in)courage, SheSeeks, *SUSIE Magazine*, from print and the Internet—your constant support and belief in me have been my strength through this publishing process. Thank you.

Huge thanks to my community of friends who stood in the gap for me, prayed for me, hugged me, and laughed often at my barely funny jokes: Betsy, Laura, Marisa, Emily, Lyndsay, Nichole, Bonesy, Clare, Brooke and Justin, Annie and Dave (and Ben), Matt and Amber (and Roxie and Ruuubes),

Matt, Barrett and Rachel, Anne, my two Jasons, Skip, Annie
P, Sonnie, Emily, Mary Katherine, Katie, Molly, Jenna, Car-
oline, Anna, Meghan, Melissa, Hillary and Chris, Kelli and
Dave, Cassie and Charles, Curt, Graham, Adam and Ansley
(and Shelbs and Blake), the Cowart family, Stunkle, Luke and
Heather, Marie-Claire, Kathleen, AeMo, Nan, the Powell family, Candace, Caren, Danielle, and Jennifer. Thanks also to the
staff at Cross Point Church in Nashville, Tennessee.

To my writing community—Denise Hildreth Jones, Shan-
non Primicerio, Sarah Markley, Linda Vujnov, Emily Freeman,
Ann Voskamp, Melanie Shankle, Sophie Hudson, Lyndsay
Rush, Angie Smith, Amanda Williams, Kelley Kirker, Ellie
Holcomb, and the (in)courage writers. Your words make me
want to be better at everything, including life. Keep on, friends.

Thanks to Corene Israel for believing in my writing from
day one (literally). I'm grateful beyond what I've ever been able
to express.

To Molly and Haley—I will never find better friends. You
always win.

To the staff at Mocha Club—what an honor to be a part.

To my students/players in Jackson County and Cherokee
County—I still know your names, and I still love you to pieces.
You were on my mind when I wrote this book. And to my
teacher friends—you are really, really good at your job. Keep
it up.

To my NanoMBAers, Seth Godin and Ishita Gupta—you
will never know how deeply you each inspire me. My life

changed that week in New York City. This book is out because you taught me how to thrash.

If I forgot to list your name, just write it in here. Please. It will make me feel better.

And I especially thank _____ for always being awesome.

To my dear glam team, who took the original book, *From Head to Foot*, and made it a gorgeous piece of art—Logan Hartline, Wes Hartline, Lyndsay Rush, Emily Keafer, Matt Lehman, Adria Haley, and to Westbow Press.

Thanks to my agent, Kyle Olund, for making this job more fun than it has ever been before. Here's to many more books and years. And thanks to the team at Zondervan. Thank you to my editor, Jacque Alberta—this book is far better because of you. I am deeply grateful.

Big thanks to Downs Books LLC (my mom and dad). Downs Books LLC is named in honor of my grandparents, Jack and Katherine Downs, who ran a rare and used bookshop for the majority of my childhood. It was open Wednesdays, Saturdays, by appointment, or by chance. I can still smell the place, hear the doorbell, and see my grandmother in her chair. The legacy they left behind—a love for good books—has hopefully lived on in this little thang. Much love to the rest of my family, and thanks to my grandmother Ruth for being a prayer warrior.

To my parents—thank you for loving me, and my dreams, far more than I know how to measure. It is a privilege to be yours. To Tatum and Sally—I strive to be a better sister because of how I see you live. Thank you for loving me. I know it ain't easy.

Finally, to You, Jesus. You saved me once, but You rescue me every single day. Whom have I but You? When my flesh and my heart fail, You are the strength of my heart and my portion. I don't know who I would be without You, and I like that. This is my worship to You.

About the Author

Annie Downs is a freelance writer in Nashville, Tennessee. Flawed but funny, she uses her writing to highlight the everyday goodness of a real and present God.

Annie has been telling stories her whole life. As a child, growing up outside of Atlanta, Georgia, she loved talking to anyone who would listen. (Actually, she still does.) Annie received her bachelor's degree in Early Childhood Education from the University of Georgia, preparing her for a short-lived but memorable career as a teacher in elementary schools. Now as a writer, Annie uses those same classroom skills to engage, entertain, and educate her readers.

With several Bible studies and many articles under her literary belt, Annie also writes books for teen girls and women braving college and the years after. Annie is passionate about seeing young women find true value in God and His love for them. By weaving together personal stories, humor, and Scripture, she invites readers to experience a fulfilled life with a living God who loves deeply.

Annie is a huge fan of the Internet, singer/songwriters, waffles with peanut butter, and sports of all kinds, especially foursquare.

Truth:

Truth:

Truth:

Lie:

Lie:

Lie:

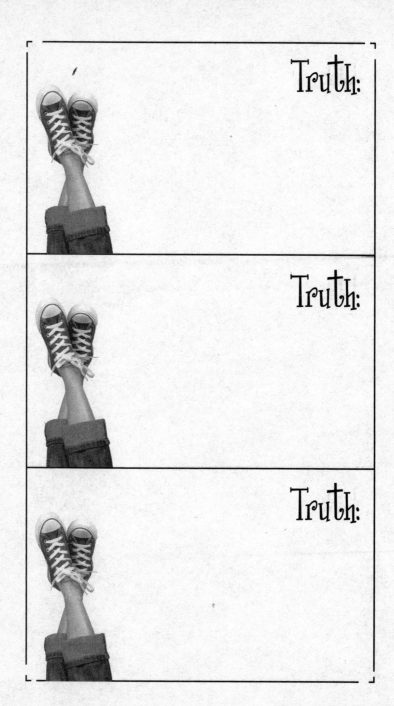

Truth:

Truth:

Truth:

Lie:

Lie:

Lie:

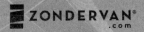